AutoCAD Release 14 For Dummies® Quick Reference

by Ellen Finkelstein

IDG Books Worldwide, Inc.
An International Data Group Company

Foster City, CA ✦ Chicago, IL ✦ Indianapolis, IN ✦ New York, NY

AutoCAD® Release 14 For Dummies® Quick Reference

Published by
IDG Books Worldwide, Inc.
An International Data Group Company
919 E. Hillsdale Blvd.
Suite 400
Foster City, CA 94404
www.idgbooks.com (IDG Books Worldwide Web site)
www.dummies.com (Dummies Press Web site)

Copyright © 1997 IDG Books Worldwide, Inc. All rights reserved. No part of this book, including interior design, cover design, and icons, may be reproduced or transmitted in any form, by any means (electronic, photocopying, recording, or otherwise) without the prior written permission of the publisher.

Library of Congress Catalog Card No.: 97-80753

ISBN: 0-7645-0316-2

Printed in the United States of America

10 9 8 7 6 5 4 3

1P/QY/QX/ZY/IN

Distributed in the United States by IDG Books Worldwide, Inc.

Distributed by Macmillan Canada for Canada; by Transworld Publishers Limited in the United Kingdom; by IDG Norge Books for Norway; by IDG Sweden Books for Sweden; by Woodslane Pty. Ltd. for Australia; by Woodslane (NZ) Ltd. for New Zealand; by Addison Wesley Longman Singapore Pte Ltd. for Singapore, Malaysia, Thailand, Indonesia and Korea; by Norma Comunicaciones S.A. for Colombia; by Intersoft for South Africa; by International Thomson Publishing for Germany, Austria and Switzerland; by Toppan Company Ltd. for Japan; by Distribuidora Cuspide for Argentina; by Livraria Cultura for Brazil; by Ediciencia S.A. for Ecuador; by Ediciones ZETA S.C.R. Ltda. for Peru; by WS Computer Publishing Corporation, Inc., for the Philippines; by Unalis Corporation for Taiwan; by Contemporanea de Ediciones for Venezuela; by Computer Book & Magazine Store for Puerto Rico; by Express Computer Distributors for the Caribbean and West Indies. Authorized Sales Agent: Anthony Rudkin Associates for the Middle East and North Africa.

For general information on IDG Books Worldwide's books in the U.S., please call our Consumer Customer Service department at 800-762-2974. For reseller information, including discounts and premium sales, please call our Reseller Customer Service department at 800-434-3422.

For information on where to purchase IDG Books Worldwide's books outside the U.S., please contact our International Sales department at 650-655-3200 or fax 650-655-3297.

For information on foreign language translations, please contact our Foreign & Subsidiary Rights department at 650-655-3021 or fax 650-655-3281.

For sales inquiries and special prices for bulk quantities, please contact our Sales department at 650-655-3200 or write to the address above.

For information on using IDG Books Worldwide's books in the classroom or for ordering examination copies, please contact our Educational Sales department at 800-434-2086 or fax 317-596-5499.

For press review copies, author interviews, or other publicity information, please contact our Public Relations department at 650-655-3000 or fax 650-655-3299.

For authorization to photocopy items for corporate, personal, or educational use, please contact Copyright Clearance Center, 222 Rosewood Drive, Danvers, MA 01923, or fax 978-750-4470.

LIMIT OF LIABILITY/DISCLAIMER OF WARRANTY: AUTHOR AND PUBLISHER HAVE USED THEIR BEST EFFORTS IN PREPARING THIS BOOK. IDG BOOKS WORLDWIDE, INC., AND AUTHOR MAKE NO REPRESENTATIONS OR WARRANTIES WITH RESPECT TO THE ACCURACY OR COMPLETENESS OF THE CONTENTS OF THIS BOOK AND SPECIFICALLY DISCLAIM ANY IMPLIED WARRANTIES OF MERCHANTABILITY OR FITNESS FOR A PARTICULAR PURPOSE. THERE ARE NO WARRANTIES WHICH EXTEND BEYOND THE DESCRIPTIONS CONTAINED IN THIS PARAGRAPH. NO WARRANTY MAY BE CREATED OR EXTENDED BY SALES REPRESENTATIVES OR WRITTEN SALES MATERIALS. THE ACCURACY AND COMPLETENESS OF THE INFORMATION PROVIDED HEREIN AND THE OPINIONS STATED HEREIN ARE NOT GUARANTEED OR WARRANTED TO PRODUCE ANY PARTICULAR RESULTS, AND THE ADVICE AND STRATEGIES CONTAINED HEREIN MAY NOT BE SUITABLE FOR EVERY INDIVIDUAL. NEITHER IDG BOOKS WORLDWIDE, INC., NOR AUTHOR SHALL BE LIABLE FOR ANY LOSS OF PROFIT OR ANY OTHER COMMERCIAL DAMAGES, INCLUDING BUT NOT LIMITED TO SPECIAL, INCIDENTAL, CONSEQUENTIAL, OR OTHER DAMAGES.

Trademarks: All brand names and product names used in this book are trade names, service marks, trademarks, or registered trademarks of their respective owners. IDG Books Worldwide is not associated with any product or vendor mentioned in this book.

is a trademark under exclusive license to IDG Books Worldwide, Inc., from International Data Group, Inc.

About the Author

Ellen Finkelstein learned AutoCAD in Israel, where she was always the one sent to pore over the manual because it was in English. After drafting and then teaching AutoCAD there, she returned to the United States and started consulting and training in AutoCAD and other computer programs, including Microsoft Word, Excel, and PowerPoint. She has been the technical editor for several books from IDG Books Worldwide, Inc. She is also an Autodesk registered author, and she wrote *AutoCAD 14 Bible* (at over 1,000 pages, it's still not as long as the real thing), was a contributing author for *AutoCAD 13 Secrets,* and has written books on Microsoft Word and PowerPoint. She writes at home so she can take the bread out of the oven on time.

ABOUT IDG BOOKS WORLDWIDE

Welcome to the world of IDG Books Worldwide.

IDG Books Worldwide, Inc., is a subsidiary of International Data Group, the world's largest publisher of computer-related information and the leading global provider of information services on information technology. IDG was founded more than 25 years ago and now employs more than 8,500 people worldwide. IDG publishes more than 275 computer publications in over 75 countries (see listing below). More than 90 million people read one or more IDG publications each month.

Launched in 1990, IDG Books Worldwide is today the #1 publisher of best-selling computer books in the United States. We are proud to have received eight awards from the Computer Press Association in recognition of editorial excellence and three from *Computer Currents'* First Annual Readers' Choice Awards. Our best-selling ...For Dummies® series has more than 50 million copies in print with translations in 38 languages. IDG Books Worldwide, through a joint venture with IDG's Hi-Tech Beijing, became the first U.S. publisher to publish a computer book in the People's Republic of China. In record time, IDG Books Worldwide has become the first choice for millions of readers around the world who want to learn how to better manage their businesses.

Our mission is simple: Every one of our books is designed to bring extra value and skill-building instructions to the reader. Our books are written by experts who understand and care about our readers. The knowledge base of our editorial staff comes from years of experience in publishing, education, and journalism — experience we use to produce books for the '90s. In short, we care about books, so we attract the best people. We devote special attention to details such as audience, interior design, use of icons, and illustrations. And because we use an efficient process of authoring, editing, and desktop publishing our books electronically, we can spend more time ensuring superior content and spend less time on the technicalities of making books.

You can count on our commitment to deliver high-quality books at competitive prices on topics you want to read about. At IDG Books Worldwide, we continue in the IDG tradition of delivering quality for more than 25 years. You'll find no better book on a subject than one from IDG Books Worldwide.

John Kilcullen
CEO
IDG Books Worldwide, Inc.

Steven Berkowitz
President and Publisher
IDG Books Worldwide, Inc.

Eighth Annual Computer Press Awards ≥1992

Ninth Annual Computer Press Awards ≥1993

Tenth Annual Computer Press Awards ≥1994

Eleventh Annual Computer Press Awards ≥1995

IDG Books Worldwide, Inc., is a subsidiary of International Data Group, the world's largest publisher of computer-related information and the leading global provider of information services on information technology. International Data Group publishes over 275 computer publications in over 75 countries. More than 90 million people read one or more International Data Group publications each month. International Data Group's publications include: **ARGENTINA:** Buyer's Guide, Computerworld Argentina, PC World Argentina; **AUSTRALIA:** Australian Macworld, Australian PC World, Australian Reseller News, Computerworld, IT Casebook, Network World, Publish, Webmaster; **AUSTRIA:** Computerwelt Osterreich, Networks Austria, PC Tip Austria; **BANGLADESH:** PC World Bangladesh; **BELARUS:** PC World Belarus; **BELGIUM:** Data News; **BRAZIL:** Annuário de Informática, Computerworld, Connections, Macworld, PC Player, PC World, Publish, Reseller News, Supergamepower; **BULGARIA:** Computerworld Bulgaria, Network World Bulgaria, PC & MacWorld Bulgaria; **CANADA:** CIO Canada, Client/Server World, ComputerWorld Canada, InfoWorld Canada, NetworkWorld Canada, WebWorld; **CHILE:** Computerworld Chile, PC World Chile; **COLOMBIA:** Computerworld Colombia, PC World Colombia; **COSTA RICA:** PC World Centro America; **THE CZECH AND SLOVAK REPUBLICS:** Computerworld Czechoslovakia, Macworld Czech Republic, PC World Czechoslovakia; **DENMARK:** Communications World Danmark, Computerworld Danmark, Macworld Danmark, PC World Danmark, Techworld Denmark; **DOMINICAN REPUBLIC:** PC World Republica Dominicana; **ECUADOR:** PC World Ecuador; **EGYPT:** Computerworld Middle East, PC World Middle East; **EL SALVADOR:** PC World Centro America; **FINLAND:** MikroPC, Tietoverkko, Tietoviikko; **FRANCE:** Distributique, Hebdo, Info PC, Le Monde Informatique, Macworld, Reseaux & Telecoms, WebMaster France; **GERMANY:** Computer Partner, Computerwoche, Computerwoche Extra, Computerwoche FOCUS, Global Online, Macwelt, PC Welt; **GREECE:** Amiga Computing, GamePro Greece, Multimedia World; **GUATEMALA:** PC World Centro America; **HONDURAS:** PC World Centro America; **HONG KONG:** Computerworld Hong Kong, PC World Hong Kong, Publish in Asia; **HUNGARY:** ABCD CD-ROM, Computerworld Szamitastechnika, Internetto online Magazine, PC World Hungary, PC-X Magazin Hungary; **ICELAND:** Tolvuheimur PC World Island; **INDIA:** Information Communications World, Information Systems Computerworld, PC World India, Publish in Asia; **INDONESIA:** InfoKomputer PC World, Komputek Computerworld, Publish in Asia; **IRELAND:** ComputerScope, PC Live!; **ISRAEL:** Macworld Israel, People & Computers/Computerworld; **ITALY:** Computerworld Italia, Macworld Italia, Networking Italia, PC World Italia; **JAPAN:** DTP World, Macworld Japan, Nikkei Personal Computing, OS/2 World Japan, SunWorld Japan, Windows NT World, Windows World Japan; **KENYA:** PC World East African; **KOREA:** Hi-Tech Information, Macworld Korea, PC World Korea; **MACEDONIA:** PC World Macedonia; **MALAYSIA:** Computerworld Malaysia, PC World Malaysia, Publish in Asia; **MALTA:** PC World Malta; **MEXICO:** Computerworld Mexico, PC World Mexico; **MYANMAR:** PC World Myanmar; **NETHERLANDS:** Computer! Totaal, LAN Internetworking Magazine, LAN World Buyers Guide, Macworld Netherlands, Net, WebWereld; **NEW ZEALAND:** Absolute Beginners Guide and Plain & Simple Series, Computer Buyer, Computer Industry Directory, Computerworld New Zealand, MTB, Network World, PC World New Zealand; **NICARAGUA:** PC World Centro America; **NORWAY:** Computerworld Norge, CW Rapport, Datamagasinet, Financial Rapport, Kursguide Norge, Macworld Norge, Multimediaworld Norge, PC World Ekspress Norge, PC World Nettverk, PC World Norge, PC World ProduktGuide Norge; **PAKISTAN:** Computerworld Pakistan; **PANAMA:** PC World Panama; **PEOPLE'S REPUBLIC OF CHINA:** China Computer Users, China Computerworld, China InfoWorld, China Telecom World Weekly, Computer & Communication, Electronic Design China, Electronics Today, Electronics Weekly, Game Software, PC World China, Popular Computer Week, Software Weekly, Software World, Telecom World; **PERU:** Computerworld Peru, PC World Profesional Peru, PC World SoHo Peru; **PHILIPPINES:** Click!, Computerworld Philippines, PC World Philippines, Publish in Asia; **POLAND:** Computerworld Poland, Computerworld Special Report Poland, Cyber, Macworld Poland, Networld Poland, PC World Komputer; **PORTUGAL:** Cerebro/PC World, Computerworld/Correio Informático, Dealer World Portugal, Mac*In/PC*In Portugal, Multimedia World; **PUERTO RICO:** PC World Puerto Rico; **ROMANIA:** Computerworld Romania, PC World Romania, Telecom Romania; **RUSSIA:** Computerworld Russia, Mir PK, Publish, Seti; **SINGAPORE:** Computerworld Singapore, PC World Singapore, Publish in Asia; **SLOVENIA:** Monitor; **SOUTH AFRICA:** Computing SA, Network World SA, Software World SA; **SPAIN:** Comunicaciones World España, Computerworld España, Dealer World España, Macworld España, PC World España; **SRI LANKA:** Infolink PC World; **SWEDEN:** CAP&Design, Computer Sweden, Corporate Computing Sweden, Internetworld Sweden, it.branschen, Macworld Sweden, MaxiData Sweden, MikroDatorn, Natverk & Kommunikation, PC World Sweden, PCaktiv, Windows World Sweden; **SWITZERLAND:** Computerworld Schweiz, Macworld Schweiz, PCtip; **TAIWAN:** Computerworld Taiwan, Macworld Taiwan, NEW VISION/Publish, PC World Taiwan, Windows World Taiwan; **THAILAND:** Publish in Asia, Thai Computerworld; **TURKEY:** Computerworld Turkiye, Macworld Turkiye, Network World Turkiye, PC World Turkiye; **UKRAINE:** Computerworld Kiev, Multimedia World Ukraine, PC World Ukraine; **UNITED KINGDOM:** Acorn User UK, Amiga Action UK, Amiga Computing UK, Apple Talk UK, Computing, Macworld, Parents and Computers UK, PC Advisor, PC Home, PSX Pro, The WEB; **UNITED STATES:** Cable in the Classroom, CIO Magazine, Computerworld, DOS World, Federal Computer Week, GamePro Magazine, InfoWorld, I-Way, Macworld, Network World, PC Games, PC World, Publish, Video Event, THE WEB Magazine, and WebMaster; online webzines: JavaWorld, NetscapeWorld, and SunWorld Online; **URUGUAY:** InfoWorld Uruguay; **VENEZUELA:** Computerworld Venezuela, PC World Venezuela; and **VIETNAM:** PC World Vietnam.

Dedication

To MMY, who taught me how to find my inner intelligence so I could write clearly — and my inner creativity so I could be funny.

Author's Acknowledgments

First, I would like to thank my husband for his incredible support while I wrote this book, which included washing innumerable clothes and dishes and putting the kids to bed every night. And thanks to my friends (and moms of my kids' friends) who helped out when I needed it. Thanks, too, to my parents for their support all my life and their belief that I could do anything (even write a book about AutoCAD, of all things). My kids didn't know they were helping, but their love, sweetness, and snugliness helped, too.

Thanks to the folks at Kibbutz Yahad, where I first learned AutoCAD. Finally, thanks to all the people at IDG Books, including Ellen Camm, Kelly Oliver, Constance Carlisle, and the folks in Production who put it all together. Thanks too to Gene Redmon, the technical editor, for doing a thorough job.

Publisher's Acknowledgments

We're proud of this book; please register your comments through our IDG Books Worldwide Online Registration Form located at: http://my2cents.dummies.com.

Some of the people who helped bring this book to market include the following:

Acquisitions, Editorial, and Media Development

Project Editor: Kelly Oliver

Acquisitions Editor: Ellen Camm

Copy Editor: Constance Carlisle

Technical Editor: Gene Redmon

Editorial Manager: Mary C. Corder

Editorial Assistant: Donna Love

Production

Project Coordinator: Sherry Gomoll

Layout and Graphics:
Lou Boudreau, Elizabeth Cárdenas-Nelson, Angela F. Hunckler, M. Anne Sipahimalani, Kate Snell, Deirdre Smith

Proofreaders: Carrie Voorhis, Michelle Croninger, Rachel Garvey, Nancy Price, Rebecca Senninger, Janet M. Withers

Indexer: Steve Rath

General and Administrative

IDG Books Worldwide, Inc.: John Kilcullen, CEO; Steven Berkowitz, President and Publisher

IDG Books Technology Publishing: Brenda McLaughlin, Senior Vice President and Group Publisher

Dummies Technology Press and Dummies Editorial: Diane Graves Steele, Vice President and Associate Publisher; Mary Bednarek, Director of Acquisitions and Product Development; Kristin A. Cocks, Editorial Director

Dummies Trade Press: Kathleen A. Welton, Vice President and Publisher; Kevin Thornton, Acquisitions Manager

IDG Books Production for Dummies Press: Michael R. Britton, Vice President of Production; Beth Jenkins Roberts, Production Director; Cindy L. Phipps, Manager of Project Coordination, Production Proofreading, and Indexing; Kathie S. Schutte, Supervisor of Page Layout; Shelley Lea, Supervisor of Graphics and Design; Debbie J. Gates, Production Systems Specialist; Robert Springer, Supervisor of Proofreading; Debbie Stailey, Special Projects Coordinator; Tony Augsburger, Supervisor of Reprints and Bluelines

Dummies Packaging and Book Design: Robin Seaman, Creative Director; Jocelyn Kelaita, Product Packaging Coordinator; Kavish + Kavish, Cover Design

♦

The publisher would like to give special thanks to Patrick J. McGovern, without whom this book would not have been possible.

♦

Table of Contents

Introduction 1

Who Needs This Book 2
How I Stuffed All of AutoCAD into This Tiny Book 2
Windows 95 and Windows NT 3
Those Little Icons 3
How This Book Is Organized 4
    Part I: The Basics 4
    Part II: The Commands 4
    Part III: The System Variables 4
    Part IV: The Menus and Toolbars 4
    Part V: Techie Talk 4

Part I: The Basics 5

Getting Started 6
    Opening a new or existing drawing 6
    The AutoCAD screen 7
    Save me, save me! 8
Ordering AutoCAD Around 9
    Pointing devices: mouse or digitizer 9
    The command line 9
    All the pretty little menus and toolbars 10
    Dialog boxes 11
It's a Setup! 11
    The template 11
    Wiz with the Wizard 12
    Units 12
    Drawing, Ltd. 12
    Layer upon layer 13
    Stylish writing 13
    Cool dimensions 13
    Creating a User Coordinate System (UCS) 14
Getting Picky: Specifying Points 14
    Displaying coordinates 15
    Oodles of coordinates 15
    Object snaps 16
    From here, there, everywhere 17
    Tracking down the elusive point 17
    Filters 18
    SNAP to it! 19
    The itsy-bitsy, teeny-weeny, yellow polka-dot grid 19
    The military meal: drawing at right angles 19
    Direct distance entry 19
Here's Lookin' at You, Kid 19

AutoCAD Release 14 For Dummies Quick Reference

Be Choosy: Selecting Objects for Editing	20
Which came first: Object or command?	20
Pick and click	21
Selection options	21
Get a grip on yourself	21
Help!	22
Get Me Out of Here!	22
Getting Keen on Release 14	23
Speed, speed, and more speed	23
ActiveX Automation: Is it a robot?	23

Part II: The Commands 25

3D	26
3DARRAY	27
3DFACE	28
3DPOLY	28
ALIGN	29
'APERTURE	29
ARC	30
AREA	30
ARRAY	30
ATTACHURL	31
ATTDEF	31
ATTDISP	31
ATTEDIT	32
ATTEXT	32
ATTREDEF	33
AUDIT	33
'BASE	33
BHATCH	34
'BLIPMODE	35
BLOCK	35
BMAKE	36
BOUNDARY	36
BOX	37
BREAK	38
BROWSER	38
'CAL	39
CHAMFER	39
CHANGE	40
CHPROP	41
CIRCLE	41
'COLOR	41
CONE	42
COPY	42
CYLINDER	43
DBLIST	43
DDATTDEF	44

DDATTE	45
DDATTEXT	46
DDCHPROP	48
DDCOLOR	48
DDEDIT	49
'DDGRIPS	49
DDIM	50
DDINSERT	51
DDMODIFY	52
'DDPTYPE	52
DDRENAME	52
'DDRMODES	53
'DDSELECT	53
DDUCS	54
DDUCSP	55
'DDUNITS	55
DDVIEW	56
DDVPOINT	57
DETACHURL	58
DIMALIGNED	58
DIMANGULAR	59
DIMBASELINE	60
DIMCENTER	60
DIMCONTINUE	61
DIMDIAMETER	61
DIMLINEAR	62
DIMRADIUS	63
DIMSTYLE	64
DIMTEDIT	64
'DIST	64
DIVIDE	65
DONUT	65
'DRAGMODE	66
DRAWORDER	66
DSVIEWER	67
DTEXT	68
DVIEW	69
DWFOUT	70
DXFIN	71
DXFOUT	72
EDGE	72
EDGESURF	73
'ELEV	73
ELLIPSE	74
ERASE	74
EXPLODE	75
EXPORT	75
EXTEND	75

EXTRUDE	76
'FILL	77
FILLET	77
'FILTER	78
'GRID	79
GROUP	80
HATCH	80
HATCHEDIT	81
HIDE	81
'ID	81
IMAGE & IMAGEATTACH	82
IMAGEADJUST	82
IMAGECLIP	82
IMAGEFRAME	83
IMAGEQUALITY	83
IMPORT	83
INETCFG	84
INSERT	84
INSERTURL	84
INTERFERE	84
INTERNET UTILITIES	85
INTERSECT	86
'ISOPLANE	87
'LAYER	87
LEADER	88
LENGTHEN	89
LIGHT	90
'LIMITS	93
LINE	94
'LINETYPE	94
LIST	95
LISTURL	96
LOGFILEOFF	96
LOGFILEON	96
'LTSCALE	96
MASSPROP	97
'MATCHPROP	97
MATLIB	98
MEASURE	98
MINSERT	99
MIRROR	99
MIRROR3D	100
MLEDIT	101
MLINE	101
MLSTYLE	102
MOVE	104
MSPACE	105
MTEXT	105
MVIEW	106

Table of Contents

MVSETUP	107
NEW	108
OFFSET	108
OOPS	109
OPEN	109
OPENURL	110
'ORTHO	110
'OSNAP	110
PAINTER	111
'PAN	111
PEDIT	111
PLAN	113
PLINE	114
PLOT	115
POINT	117
POLYGON	117
PREFERENCES	118
PSPACE	119
PURGE	120
QSAVE	120
'QTEXT	121
QUIT	121
RAY	121
RECOVER	122
RECTANG	122
REDO	123
'REDRAWALL	123
REGEN	124
REGENAUTO	124
REGION	124
REINIT	125
RENAME	125
RENDER	125
REVOLVE	127
REVSURF	128
RMAT	129
ROTATE	131
ROTATE3D	131
RPREF	132
RULESURF	132
SAVE	133
SAVEAS	133
SAVEIMG	133
SAVEURL	134
SCALE	134
SCENE	134
SECTION	135
SELECT	136
SELECTURL	137

'SETVAR	138
SHADE	138
SKETCH	139
SLICE	139
'SNAP	140
SOLID	141
'SPELL	141
SPHERE	142
SPLINE	142
SPLINEDIT	143
STATS	145
'STATUS	145
STRETCH	145
'STYLE	146
SUBTRACT	147
TABLET	147
TABSURF	149
TEXT	149
'TIME	149
TOLERANCE	150
TOOLBAR	151
TORUS	152
TRACE	153
TRANSPARENCY	153
TRIM	153
U	154
UCS	154
UCSICON	156
UNDO	156
UNION	157
'UNITS	157
'VIEW	157
VIEWRES	158
VPLAYER	158
VPOINT	160
VPORTS	161
WBLOCK	162
WEDGE	163
XCLIP	163
XLINE	164
XPLODE	164
XREF & XATTACH	165
'ZOOM	167

Part III: The System Variables 169

Using System Variables	170
3D	170
Attributes	171

Table of Contents

```
        Dimensioning .................................................................. 171
        Drawing Aids ................................................................ 172
        Edits ................................................................................ 173
        Information/Customization ........................................ 173
        Object Creation ............................................................ 175
        Text .................................................................................. 176
```

Part IV: The Menus and Toolbars 177

```
    Using Menus and Toolbars .................................................. 178
    AutoCAD Menus .................................................................. 179
        The File menu .............................................................. 179
        The Edit menu ............................................................. 179
        The View menu ........................................................... 179
        The Insert menu ......................................................... 181
        The Format menu ...................................................... 182
        The Tools menu .......................................................... 182
        The Draw menu .......................................................... 183
        The Dimension menu ................................................ 185
        The Modify menu ....................................................... 185
        The Help menu ........................................................... 186
    AutoCAD Toolbars ............................................................... 186
        The Standard toolbar ................................................ 186
        The Object Snap flyout/toolbar ............................. 187
        The UCS flyout/toolbar ............................................ 187
        The Inquiry flyout/toolbar ..................................... 188
        The Viewpoint flyout/toolbar ................................ 188
        The Zoom flyout/toolbar ......................................... 188
        The Object Properties toolbar .............................. 189
        The Draw toolbar ....................................................... 189
        The Insert flyout/toolbar ........................................ 190
        The Modify toolbar .................................................... 190
        The External Reference toolbar ............................ 190
        The Dimension toolbar ............................................ 191
        The Modify II toolbar ............................................... 191
        The Reference toolbar ............................................. 192
        The Render toolbar ................................................... 192
        The Solids toolbar ..................................................... 193
        The Surfaces toolbar ................................................ 193
        The Internet Utilities toolbar ................................ 193
```

Part V: Techie Talk 195

Index 201

Book Registration Information ...... Back of Book

How to Use This Book

Hi! I'm Nobody! Who are you?

Are you nobody, too?

Then there's a pair of us — don't tell!

They'd banish us, you know.

　　　　　—Emily Dickinson

This book is for us nobodies (or us Dummies) — normal people who want or need to use AutoCAD without having to be an engineer or a programmer. (Even those engineers and programmers among you must have a normal side!) Sure, AutoCAD is complex, but it doesn't have to be scary. This book organizes a vast amount of information about AutoCAD for you, so that you can read only the parts that you need. You can stay blissfully unaware of the rest and still get your job done.

2 How to Use This Book

Who Needs This Book

This book is useful for beginning and advanced AutoCAD users, as well as for most of you who fall somewhere in the middle. The book covers the vast majority of commands in Release 14, including how to use each command and what those obscure AutoCAD terms mean. *AutoCAD Release 14 For Dummies Quick Reference* is loaded with icons that tell you how useful or safe a command is, tips that enable you to get more out of AutoCAD, and warnings that tell you when to be careful.

AutoCAD Release 14 For Dummies Quick Reference is, as the name implies, a reference book. You probably should know just a little about AutoCAD first. A great place to start is with *AutoCAD Release 14 For Dummies* by Bud Smith (IDG Books Worldwide, Inc.); it's informative, chock-full of good advice, easy to read, and (most importantly) funny! When you're ready for a full-length, comprehensive reference, I'm not too shy to recommend my own tome, *AutoCAD 14 Bible*, also published by IDG Books Worldwide, Inc.

After you start using AutoCAD, this book is the one to keep by your computer all the time. No one can know everything about AutoCAD, so you'll always need to look things up. That's okay. Really! (Now that you know the secret — that even advanced users continue to look up things about AutoCAD — you won't feel so self-conscious when you do it.)

How I Stuffed All of AutoCAD into This Tiny Book

I actually included almost all the AutoCAD commands, including all the regular 2D, 3D, and rendering commands. What did I leave out? Well, because this book is a Quick Reference, I felt that I couldn't do justice to some subjects in a short format. Those subjects are the commands related to LISP (AutoCAD's programming language), importing and exporting other types of files, customizing AutoCAD (such as writing script files or customizing menus), and the AutoCAD SQL Environment (ASE) commands. There's no point doing a bad job of describing something, so I left those subjects out, as well as a couple of others that are very rarely used.

Also, I covered each command only briefly (remember, this book is a reference, not a long-winded technical explanation). I tell you *how* to use the command by walking you through the options, suboptions, and sometimes sub-suboptions.

How to Use This Book   3

Windows 95 and Windows NT

The first edition of this book covered DOS and Windows versions of AutoCAD, but I warned that Windows was taking over the world. Prescient remark, that. AutoCAD now operates only under (or over) Windows 95 and Windows NT. However, upgrading from a DOS version is easy. When it comes down to the nitty-gritty, AutoCAD always reverts to the command line — and that, dear reader, is the same for Windows as it was for DOS.

Those Little Icons

Following are the icons I use in the book. These icons can give you an instant impression of a topic, so you can decide whether it's the one that you want.

This book covers some advanced commands and technical stuff. This icon informs you before you take the plunge.

On the other hand, some commands are easy as pie. This icon tells you that you can take a sigh of relief.

I use this icon to provide some additional information that you need to pay special attention to.

This icon indicates features that are new or significantly changed in Release 14.

This icon warns you of problem areas that can mess up your work.

This icon points out clever AutoCAD tricks to help you along the way.

This icon directs you to more details in *AutoCAD Release 14 For Dummies* by Bud Smith (IDG Books Worldwide, Inc.).

I use this icon only a couple of times. I still have a little shame. It refers you to my other book on AutoCAD and other books published by IDG Books Worldwide, Inc.

4 *How to Use This Book*

How This Book Is Organized

Because this is a reference book, the material is organized for easy look-up. The headings help you to quickly find what you need to know. And although your sixth-grade teacher probably told you not to do this, I give you permission to fold down the corner of any pages you want.

Part I: The Basics

This part gives you the basics that you can't find under any command. The part includes brief sections on getting started, using commands, setting up a drawing, specifying points, viewing your drawing, selecting objects, organizing your drawing with layers, using Help and Learning Assistance, and getting in and out of drawings safely and efficiently. As necessary, I refer you to the appropriate command in Part II. I also talk a bit about some of the exciting new developments in Release 14 such as support for ActiveX Automation.

Part II: The Commands

This part is an alphabetical listing of all (well, almost all) the commands. I don't expect you to read this part through from beginning to end — although it's okay if you want to. Part II is the main reference section; just look up the command that you need.

Part III: The System Variables

Part III lists the system variables not controlled using any command and a few especially useful system variables. As AutoCAD slowly improves its interface, more of the system variables are handled in dialog boxes, but you still may want to type some of them in the command line. I organized these variables by function so that you can find them easily.

Part IV: The Menus and Toolbars

If you know that you want to do some task but don't know the command name, you can look in this part. The menus and toolbars are organized by type of task (Draw, Modify, and so on).

Part V: Techie Talk

You've heard of Newspeak (from George Orwell's *1984*)? Well, AutoCAD has AutoSpeak. Actually, I have to thank Autodesk because some of my best jokes in this book came from the absurdity of the terminology used in AutoCAD. In the glossary, I include words that have unique meanings in the AutoCAD world — often meanings quite different from what their names suggest.

The Basics

If you're a new AutoCAD user, be sure to read this part; you find out how to get started and review the basics that you need to understand the unique world of AutoCAD. If you're already familiar with AutoCAD, you may want to skim through; you know most of this stuff, but you're sure to find something new. At the very least, look for the Release 14 icons to get yourself up to speed on the latest and the greatest.

Throughout this part, I refer as necessary to commands listed in Part II of this book.

In this part . . .

- ✔ Looking at the AutoCAD screen
- ✔ Ordering AutoCAD around
- ✔ Setting up a drawing
- ✔ Specifying coordinates
- ✔ Selecting objects for editing
- ✔ Getting help

Getting Started

It's good to start at the beginning, and you start by launching AutoCAD. After installing AutoCAD, you can start by choosing Start➪Programs➪AutoCAD R14. However, sharp operators know that opening AutoCAD from a shortcut on the desktop is easier. To create a shortcut, follow these steps:

1. Double-click My Computer from the desktop and find acad.exe. It's probably in the AutoCAD R14 folder.

2. Right-click it.

3. Choose Make Shortcut. You see a new icon that says *shortcut to acad.exe*.

4. Drag the icon to your desktop.

5. Click the icon's name and type in any new name you want. Press Enter.

You can now double-click the icon to open AutoCAD. Much better!

See Appendix A of *AutoCAD Release 14 For Dummies* by Bud Smith (published by IDG Books Worldwide, Inc.) for some help on installing AutoCAD.

Opening a new or existing drawing

When you start AutoCAD, you see the Start Up dialog box with four choices:

+ **Use a Wizard.** Walks you through the process of setting up a drawing, covered later in this part.

+ **Use a Template.** Enables you to choose a template as a basis for a new drawing. Templates used to be called prototypes, but the the two are pretty much the same thing — except that they have their own file type (the file extension is .dwt). Templates are covered later in this chapter, too.

+ **Start from Scratch.** Enables you to start a new drawing with only the basic default settings.

+ **Open a Drawing.** Enables you to choose an existing drawing to work on.

You can also choose Instructions to get help on the four choices.

Whichever you choose, you find yourself magically transported into a new or existing drawing. You can click your heels to get home or just start drawing.

Getting Started 7

After you've worked on a drawing, you can open a new drawing by clicking New on the Standard toolbar. You can open an existing drawing by clicking Open on the Standard toolbar.

See also the OPEN and the NEW commands in Part II.

The AutoCAD screen

Here's the way your screen looks when you open AutoCAD.

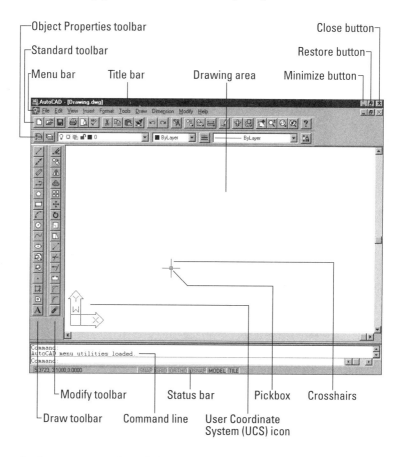

At the very top is the title bar that tells you that you're in AutoCAD (in case you were confused) and gives you the name of your drawing. If you've opened a new drawing and haven't named it yet, the title bar lists the drawing as Drawing.dwg.

The next row is the menu bar. Use the menus in this bar to choose commands.

8 Getting Started

Below the menu bar is the Standard toolbar. This toolbar contains many of the most commonly used commands. The Object Properties toolbar comes next. Use it to control layers, linetypes, and colors. On the left of the screen, you see the Draw and Modify toolbars.

You, the magician, can make many more toolbars appear by using the TOOLBAR command. Some toolbars have secondary menus called *flyouts*; you find them by clicking any icon that has a little black arrow in the corner and holding down the mouse button until they fly out (or dragging the pointer to the side of the menu).

The big space in the middle is where you draw. Here you see a small crosshair with a pickbox at its center. The crosshairs represents the cursor while you are drawing.

The small crosshairs is new for Release 14. But if you're used to the full-screen crosshair, choose Tools➪Preferences and then choose the Pointer tab. Under percentage of Screen Size, specify 100 to work the old-fashioned way.

Below the drawing area is the command line where you can type commands, options, and values such as the length of a radius.

The status bar is at the bottom. The snap, grid, and ortho indicators double as buttons; double-click to turn them on and off. The same goes for the model button (to toggle between model and paper space) and the tile button (to turn tilemode on and off). That's cool. (Clicking only once would be cooler, but the double-click is a Windows standard.)

Release 14 has added the OSNAP button on the status bar. This button turns your running object snaps on and off. For more details, see the section "Object snaps" later in this part.

Save me, save me!

It may seem funny for me to talk about saving before I talk about drawing anything, but it's never too early to find out how to save. Use the QSAVE command (click Save on the Standard toolbar) frequently to save your drawing. The first time you save a new, unnamed drawing, AutoCAD opens a dialog box so that you can name it. Furthermore, I recommend setting AutoCAD to save your drawing automatically at regular intervals. You know that the only time you forget to save is right before your computer crashes. Choose Options➪Preferences and click the General tab of the Preferences dialog box. Check the Automatic Save check box and type the time interval you want. The default is a ridiculous 120 minutes. Whoever thought you wouldn't mind redoing two hours of work if AutoCAD crashes is just a little nuts. Change the setting to 15 or 30 minutes — max.

Ordering AutoCAD Around

I don't know what the AutoCAD menus do at night when we're not looking, but they do seem to multiply. AutoCAD has the screen menu, the menu bar, the tablet menu, the button menu, the cursor menu, and the toolbars. And, of course, there's the ever-present command line, which you can use if you hate menus.

Pointing devices: mouse or digitizer

Most people use a mouse with AutoCAD. Some people use a digitizing tablet, which works with a *puck* or *stylus*. Technically, *digitizing* means copying a paper drawing with the stylus on the tablet, point by point. People sometimes use this method to convert paper drawings to computerized ones. You can use the digitizing tablet as a menu as well; in fact, AutoCAD comes with a sample tablet template.

The left button on your mouse is the *pick* button, which means that you pick things with it — a menu item, a toolbar button, or an object that you've drawn. The right button is the *Return* button, which means that clicking it is the same thing as pressing the Enter key on your keyboard. If your mouse has more than two buttons, try them out to see what they do. You may like what you find.

The command line

You can enter all commands at the command line just by typing them at the command line at the bottom of the screen. So even though Part II tells you how to access each command using a menu or toolbar, you can always type the command name in the command line. Try as you may, you can't get away from the command line completely. Often, a command that starts with a dialog box or a button reverts to the command line for you to input coordinates, values, or command options.

Options are listed along the command line, separated by slashes (/). One or more letters of the option are capitalized. You need type only the capitalized letter or letters to choose the option (but you can type in lowercase letters). The command's default, if any, appears in angled brackets (< >). Press Enter to choose the default.

Every time you need to type something at the command line — such as the name of a command, an option, coordinates, or values — you must press Enter afterward.

Transparent commands are commands that you can type at the command line while you're in the middle of another command. These commands appear in Part II preceded by an apostrophe (')

Ordering AutoCAD Around

because that's how you type them if you want to use these commands transparently. Suppose that you have snap on, and you select an object to move. When you need to specify where to move the object, however, you need to turn the snap off. Type **'snap** at the command line, press Enter, type **off**, and press Enter again. Then your MOVE command continues, and you can complete the command.

The buttons on the status bar also function as transparent commands.

After you use a command, you can repeat it by pressing Enter. If you start a command and change your mind, press the Esc key.

You can use the F2 key to open the text screen and see more of the command-line history. Pressing F2 again gets you back to the drawing screen.

At long last, Autodesk has made the command line editable. If you type out a complex coordinate and see that you've made a mistake, you don't have to type the whole darn thing over. Just use the arrow keys to move back to the mistake. Use either the Backspace key to erase your entry to the left of the cursor or the Del key to erase your entry to the right of the cursor. To repeat the previous command line entry, press the Up arrow and then press Enter.

All the pretty little menus and toolbars

Using the mouse to start commands in AutoCAD is convenient. You're looking at the screen as you draw, and you don't need to look down at the keyboard or anywhere else. The commands are right there, where you're drawing. In this book, I ignore the hallowed screen menu (AutoCAD's first menu) and direct you to the menu bar and toolbars.

The menus are easy to use. An ellipsis (...) after an item means that the item opens a dialog box. An arrow means that suboptions pop out from the item. The nice items with nothing after them execute a command for you without any further delay.

You can use the keyboard to access a menu. Hold down the Alt key and press whichever letter is underlined in the menu. Then press the letter that is underlined on the item you want. Most people use the mouse.

AutoCAD also has a cursor menu, which you get to by pressing the Shift key and clicking the Return (right) button of your mouse. The menu is called a cursor menu because it pops up at the cursor. By default, the menu offers you object snaps and point filters. If you're into that sort of stuff, you can customize this menu (and all other menus, as well).

A word about toolbars: You can't use AutoCAD efficiently without knowing how to use the toolbars. Most toolbars are hidden until you command them to show themselves (by using the TOOLBAR command, which is covered in Part II).

See also Part IV for the complete set of menus and toolbars.

Dialog boxes

Some commands open dialog boxes. Usually, these dialog boxes are fairly simple to understand. They're often easier to understand than the same operation on the command line. Choose the options you want and click OK. (Sometimes the button says Save or Open.) Some dialog boxes offer image tiles that enable you to see the results of your choices. When I have the choice of using a dialog box or the command line, I go with the dialog box.

If you like to use the keyboard, dialog boxes have underlined letters that you can use to get to an option. Most people find using the mouse to be easier than using the keyboard. Don't forget the Help button, which explains each dialog box option (although not always very thoroughly). Also, many dialog boxes have a question mark at the top right corner. To get help on any item in a dialog box, click the question mark, and then the item.

It's a Setup!

This section explains how to set up a drawing. AutoCAD is famous for the extent of its customizability — this setup is just one example. Before you draw, you need to make some preparations for efficient drawing, and that's what this section is all about.

The template

When you open a new drawing using the Use a Template option, AutoCAD asks you to choose a template. (Templates used to be called *prototype drawings*.) The default template is acad.dwt. You can change the settings of this template to whatever you want. Most offices have standards for the majority of these settings. Using a template is a great time-saver, because you don't have to create these settings every time you start a new drawing. For example, you can create layers (with the LAYER command), set drawing limits (with the LIMITS command), and create text and dimension styles (with the STYLE and DDIM commands). To customize acad.dwt or create a new template, follow these steps:

   1. Open a new drawing using the Start from Scratch option if you don't want any extraneous settings. Or open an existing

It's a Setup!

drawing that has most or all the settings you want. (If you use an existing drawing, erase any unwanted objects.) You can use the Wizard option if you want.

2. Create the settings you want, by either using the Wizard or the individual commands.

3. Choose File⇨Save if you're in a new drawing. Choose File⇨Save As, if you're working from an existing, named drawing.

4. In the Save Drawing As dialog box, click the Save as type drop-down arrow. Choose Drawing Template File (*.dwt).

5. The dialog box lists the current templates in the \Template folder. If you want to customize acad.dwt or another existing template, choose it. Otherwise, give your template a new name in the File name text box.

6. Click Save.

To use the template, choose Use a Template in the Startup dialog box, choose your template and click OK. (You may have to navigate folders to find it.)

You can create several templates. You may want to insert a title block and border for each size of drawing that you use. That way, when you start a new drawing, everything is set up for you.

Wiz with the Wizard

When you start AutoCAD, pick Use a Wizard to bring you through the process of setting up a drawing. You can choose a quick setup to choose only your unit of measurement type and drawing limits. Choose the advanced setup to include drawing layout and paper space options. You can also use individual commands to create the same effect as explained in the next few sections. Save all these settings in your template.

Units

If you don't use the Wizard when you set up a drawing, one of the first things that you may want to use is the DDUNITS command. With this command, you decide such basics as whether your measurements will be in decimals, or in feet and inches, and how precisely the measurements will be displayed. You can also set your units of measurement for angles.

Drawing, Ltd.

Another basic setup item is the drawing limits that set the basic size of your drawing. Usually, you draw life-size and then scale your drawing when you plot. *See also* the LIMITS command.

Layer upon layer

Layers are *very* important. They organize the objects in your drawings by color and linetype (continuous, dotted, dashed, and so on). Layers make sure that all dimensions have the same color or all center lines use the same color and linetype so your drawing is easier to understand. If you use AutoCAD at work, your office probably has standards for layers so that all drawings use the same layers for the same types of objects. Write down these standards and make them available to everyone. Create layers using the LAYER command (choose Layer from the Object Properties toolbar).

After you define your layers, you can make a layer current by choosing it from the Layer Control drop-down list on the Object Properties toolbar.

A new way to change the current layer is to pick an object that's on the layer you want to make current. Then click Make Object's Layer Current on the Object Properties toolbar.

With Release 14, the Object Properties toolbar works somewhat like the Formatting toolbar on your word processor. When no object is selected, the Layer, Color, and Linetype Control drop-down lists display the current layer, color, and linetype. But, when an object is selected, the Object Properties toolbar displays the layer, color, and linetype of the selected object.

Stylish writing

When the time comes to annotate your drawing, you need to get into text styles. Your office may have some standards regarding text styles — you don't want some drawings using a plain font and others using a font with lots of curlicues.

Create text styles with the STYLE command. When you create a style, it becomes the current style. The DTEXT and MTEXT commands have a Style option so that you can specify the style before you type your text.

Cool dimensions

Dimension styles are very complex. You're lucky if someone else has gone through all those dialog boxes and created a dimension style for you. If not, look up the DDIM command in Part II. Then use any of the dimension commands (all of them start with DIM . . .) to start creating dimensions.

14 Getting Picky: Specifying Points

Creating a User Coordinate System (UCS)

If you're into 3D, you can set up your coordinates anywhere and in any direction you want. (You can do so for a 2D drawing, but it's not as necessary.) If you're drawing an angled roof for a house, you can set the origin to the bottom-left corner of the roof and angle the X,Y coordinates so that they match the edges and angle of the roof. That procedure makes drawing a skylight in the roof a lot easier. *See also* the UCS command in Part II.

After you create a UCS, you can save it for later use. (Or you can use one of the AutoCAD preset UCSs. *See also* DDUCSP.) After you have your UCS, all coordinates are based on the origin and axes that you defined in your UCS.

Getting Picky: Specifying Points

You're going to spend a lot of time specifying coordinates of the objects that you draw. Coordinates are based on a Cartesian coordinate system, with X and Y (and Z, for 3D) axes. Positive numbers go to the right and up from the origin (0,0,0); negative numbers (because of their sins) go in the other direction. The universal convention for specifying coordinates is to type the X coordinate first, then a comma, and then the Y coordinate. The figure shows a few coordinates.

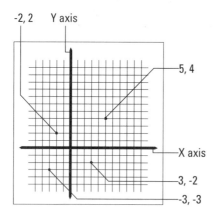

You can specify coordinates in several ways. The simplest way is to pick a point on-screen with your mouse. But that method may not be the most accurate. Often, you need to type coordinates to get the precision that you need.

Getting Picky: Specifying Points 15

Displaying coordinates

Before you start typing coordinates, knowing where you are helps. AutoCAD helpfully displays coordinates in the status bar. AutoCAD has three types of coordinate display: *static,* which shows only points that you specify; *dynamic,* which moves as the cursor moves; and *distance<angle,* which also moves as the cursor moves. The distance<angle display appears only while you're using a command in which you need to specify more than one point. Examples are drawing a line or moving an object. You toggle among these displays by pressing the F6 key or Ctrl+D. Get into the habit of looking at those coordinates so that you don't get lost!

Oodles of coordinates

You can use five types of coordinates; as you get used to them, you know which is the right one to use in your particular situation. Two types of coordinates are used only for 3D.

Absolute Cartesian coordinates are called *absolute* because they're based on the X,Y coordinate system. The point is (no pun intended — well, maybe I did intend a little . . .) that absolute coordinates are relative to the 0,0 point of your X and Y axes — as in 3,4. If drawing in 3D, add the Z axis coordinate.

Often you don't know the absolute coordinate, but you know the change in X and Y from your last point, such as the start point of the line that you're drawing. Here's where *relative Cartesian coordinates* can help. Relative coordinates are relative to the last point that you drew. You tell AutoCAD that you're using a relative coordinate by typing the @ symbol in front of the coordinates, as in @3,4. (You can find that symbol on the 2 key on your keyboard, and you need to press the Shift key to get it. Why the creators of AutoCAD picked something that's so hard to type, I'll never know.) If you're drawing in 3D, all you do is add the Z-axis coordinate.

Very often, all you know is how long your line is supposed to be and in what direction it should go. *Polar coordinates* to the rescue! Polar coordinates can be both relative and absolute. These coordinates define a point in terms of a distance (the length of your line, for example) and an angle.

The format for polar coordinates is *length<angle,* as in 6<30. Relative polar coordinates are measured relative to the last point that you drew and require the @ symbol.

Zero degrees runs along the positive X axis, and angles are measured counterclockwise from there. (If you're into weird angle measurements, you can change how they're measured by using the DDUNITS command.) You can type negative angles to measure clockwise, so that –90 degrees is the same as 270 degrees.

16 Getting Picky: Specifying Points

Cylindrical coordinates are the 3D version of polar coordinates. (If 3D drafting makes you run in the opposite direction, just skip this section.) They can also be absolute or relative. Cylindrical coordinates can also be confusing. That's because the lengths don't indicate the length of the line (or whatever you're drawing), as polar coordinates do, but the number of units in a certain direction.

The format for cylindrical coordinates is *distance<angle,distance,* as in 6<30,4. The first distance is the number of units in the XY plane. The angle is the number of degrees from the X axis in the XY plane. With these two points, you have defined a point on the XY plane. Now comes the last distance, the number of units along the Z axis, which defines the point in three dimensions. (Don't forget to use the @ symbol if you're specifying the coordinate relative to the last point that you entered.)

Spherical coordinates are like cylindrical ones, except that instead of a second distance, you use a second angle. Got it?

The format for spherical coordinates is *distance<angle<angle,* as in 6<30<45. The distance is the number of units from the origin or your last point. The first angle is the angle from the X axis in the XY plane. The second angle is the angle up from the XY plane (in the Z direction). Spherical coordinates indicate the actual distance so that a line drawn from 0,0 to 6<30<45 is 6 units long. Use the @ symbol for relative spherical coordinates.

Object snaps

If the coordinate that you want is on an object, you often can use *object snaps,* which are geometric points on objects. For example, you can move the endpoint of one line to the midpoint of another using object snaps. Anytime AutoCAD asks you for a point, you can use an object snap. You can use an object snap for one command, or you can set running object snaps that continue until you turn them off. See the OSNAP command (that's object snaps in AutoSpeak) for details on setting running snaps.

You can choose an object snap in several ways. Probably the best way is to use the Cursor menu (press Shift and click the Return button). Also, the Standard toolbar has an Object Snap flyout that contains icons for each object snap type. If you're typing coordinates anyway, you can type the object snap abbreviation. (Try typing the first three letters; that method usually works.)

The objects snaps are *endpoint, midpoint, intersection, apparent intersection, center, quadrant, node, insertion, perpendicular, tangent, nearest, quick,* and *none.* Obviously, some objects snaps are appropriate only for certain objects. Only circles, arcs, and ellipses have a center, for example. *Insertion* means the insertion point in text and blocks.

Getting Picky: Specifying Points   17

New for Release 14 is AutoSnap which lets you know when you're near an object snap that you've turned on (by setting it as a running object snap or choosing it just for the current command). You see a Snap Tip that labels the object snap and a marker that shows the location of the object snap. Each object snap has its own marker shape. There's also a magnetic pull that draws the cursor to the object snap that it loves. If you want a specific object snap and several are in the neighborhood, press Tab repeatedly to cycle through the object snaps. You can now use the OSNAP button on the status bar to turn running object snaps on and off instantly. This convenient OSNAP button makes it easier than in previous AutoCAD releases to use running object snaps all the time — turning them off is just a double-click away. Then double-click to turn them back on.

From here, there, everywhere

But what if the point you want to specify isn't on an object, but near it? *From* isn't really an object snap, although you can find it in all the same places that object snaps lurk. The From feature is a way to specify a point that's a certain distance (called an offset) from a point you can more easily specify. Say that you have two existing lines and want to start a new line at the point in the middle of the figure.

Start the LINE command, and at the From point: prompt, choose From from the cursor menu (don't let that double from fool you). You can also find it on the Object Snap flyout of the Standard toolbar or you can simply type it on the command line. AutoCAD asks you for a base point. In this case, you can use the intersection object snap to pick the intersection of the existing lines. AutoCAD asks you for the offset. If the line is supposed to start 1 unit to the right and 1 unit up from the base point, type @1,1. (You can use any type of relative coordinates.) AutoCAD starts the line right where you want it and you can now finish your line.

Tracking down the elusive point

Tracking is a new feature that enables you to locate a new point based on the coordinates of object snaps on existing objects. This

Getting Picky: Specifying Points

feature is a way to track down coordinates and capture them to create a new coordinate. It's only meant for 2D drafting. In the figure, say that you want to draw a line from the point.

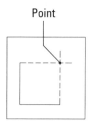
Point

Do you see how the point has the same X coordinate as the horizontal line and the same Y coordinate as the vertical line? Another way to look at it is to consider two imaginary lines perpendicular to each of the existing lines (shown by the dashed lines). These lines would intersect right at the point you want. To use Tracking, start a command (in this case, the LINE command) and when AutoCAD asks you for a point, choose Tracking (you can find it wherever object snaps are sold). At the First tracking point: prompt, use an object snap (usually) to specify the first point that has a coordinate you want to capture, such as the right endpoint of the horizontal line. Now move the cursor in the direction of the desired point (that's important) and at the Next point: prompt use an object snap to specify the second point (here the top endpoint of the other line). Press Enter to end tracking and AutoCAD locates the point you want. Mission accomplished!

Filters

Point filters enable you to extract all or part of a coordinate from an object. This capability helps when the coordinate that you need isn't obvious. (Yes, it's similar to tracking. It's slower but sometimes more precise. And it's a necessity for 3D drawing.) The format is a period (.) and one or two axis letters. Whichever filter you use, AutoCAD prompts you for the *other* axis value(s).

Using the same figure as in the Tracking section, start the LINE command. At the From point: prompt, type **.x** and then press Enter. AutoCAD responds with the of prompt, meaning, "What do you want to find the X coordinate of?" In this example, you use an endpoint object snap to pick the right endpoint of the existing horizontal line. Now AutoCAD responds with the (need YZ): prompt. Pick the endpoint of the existing vertical line. (Ignore the request for a Z coordinate if you're drawing in 2D only.) AutoCAD locates your point and you can continue to draw your line.

SNAP to it!

Turning on snap restricts the cursor to points on an invisible grid. When you turn on snap, you set the size of the grid. If you turn on snap at .5, for example, the cursor jumps to points every half-unit apart; anything in between is off-limits.

If your drawing has lots of complex coordinates, such as (3.165,4.2798), snap won't help you. But if you use simpler coordinates, such as (3.25,6.5), snap is for you. Turning on snap enables you to draw without typing coordinates. You just watch those coordinates in the status bar and, when you have the coordinates you need, click to pick the point. This method is fast and accurate. **See also** the SNAP and DDRMODES in Part II for details.

The itsy-bitsy, teeny-weeny, yellow polka-dot grid

Okay, so it's not yellow; it's grayish. The grid is a rectangular array of dots that you can turn on to help you get your bearings. Usually, you want to set the grid equal to the snap. **See also** GRID and DDRMODES in Part II for further information.

The military meal: drawing at right angles

Many things in life are at right angles. Walls and doors are at right angles from the floor (otherwise, the house comes tumbling down). ORTHO stands for orthogonal and enables you to draw at right angles only. Like snap, ORTHO (in the right situation) can increase drawing speed and accuracy. You can double-click ORTHO on and off from the status bar. **See also** ORTHO and DDRMODES in Part II.

Direct distance entry

Direct distance entry is a shortcut way to enter a polar coordinate. If you know the distance, move the cursor in the direction that you want to go to indicate the angle and then type the distance only. Direct distance entry works best in orthogonal mode because that way you can control the direction of the cursor. For example, to draw a line that is six units in the 90 degree direction, pick a start point and at the To point: prompt, move the cursor in the 90 degree direction (up), type **6**, and press Enter.

Here's Lookin' at You, Kid

After you draw something, you often need to *zoom* in closer to see the fine detail of your masterpiece and then zoom out again to see

20 Be Choosy: Selecting Objects for Editing

the drawing as a whole. The ZOOM command has many helpful options. This command is indispensable, so be sure to look it up in Part II. *See also* DSVIEWER, which opens the Aerial Viewer.

Release 14 introduces real-time Zoom which enables you to zoom in and out as you move the cursor. Check it out under ZOOM in Part II.

When you zoom in, you may find that you want to move a little to the right (or left, or whatever). *Panning* enables you to move from place to place in your drawing. You also can use the scroll bars to pan at right angles.

Real-time pan comes hand in hand with real-time zoom. Look up the PAN command in Part II.

The REDRAW and REGEN commands refresh the drawing screen. The REGEN command also recomputes coordinates, reindexes the database, and so on.

If you're drawing in 3D, you want to view your drawing from different angles. You can look at your 3D drawing from any angle, even from below (I call that the gopher view). Use the DDVPOINT or VPOINT commands. Both commands set the viewing angle, but in different ways. Pick the method that's most meaningful for you.

Obviously, part of looking at your drawing involves plotting it. Look up the PLOT command for details. You also may want to check out the concept of *paper space,* which is a way of setting up a drawing for plotting. Paper space is most useful for 3D drawings, because it enables you to create floating viewports, each with a different view of your objects. But even 2D drawings can benefit from paper space. The procedure is a bit complex, but hey! — this is AutoCAD. Look up the following commands: PSPACE, MSPACE, and MVIEW.

Be Choosy: Selecting Objects for Editing

No one ever drew a drawing without making any mistakes. You always need to edit. Even the basic drawing process often involves copying or mirroring objects. Along with the editing process comes the need to select which objects to edit.

Which came first: Object or command?

When you want to make changes, you need to know two things: Which command to use and which objects to change. Traditionally, AutoCAD required you to enter a command first and then select the objects. However, the Windows tradition is to select objects first and then apply the command to those objects. The DDSELECT command enables you to customize the way you select objects.

Be Choosy: Selecting Objects for Editing 21

AutoCAD, in true AutoSpeak, calls the concept of selecting the objects first and the command second *Noun/Verb Selection.* You see, the object that you're selecting is a thing, which is a *noun.* (You never thought of your circles as being nouns?) The command carries out an action, so it's a *verb.* The only good thing about all this nonsense is that if you choose Noun/Verb Selection (which you can do with the DDSELECT command), you get the best of two worlds: AutoCAD accepts object selection first or second, whichever you want. So choosing the option pays.

As an exercise in AutoSpeak, try turning your editing operations into little sentences, according to whether you select objects first or second. *I move a circle. A circle I move.* (I don't advise you to do this out loud, if other people are around.)

Note that some commands don't accept object selection first, no matter what you choose with the DDSELECT command. Don't worry, if you try to select objects first with these commands and nothing happens, you soon figure it out.

You also can use the SELECT command, which simply selects objects. Then you start a command and, at the `Select objects` prompt, type **p**, which stands for *previous.* All the objects that you choose during the SELECT command are highlighted and ready for action.

Pick and click

When you choose an editing command, you usually see the `Select objects` prompt. The crosshairs turn into a *pickbox,* which is a little box for picking objects. Move that box over the object that you want to pick and then click.

Selection options

You can select objects in other ways, too. For example, you can create windows (or fences or polygons) around objects and then select everything inside the window. These methods are especially good for selecting many objects at the same time. ***See also*** the SELECT command for details.

Get a grip on yourself

Grips are little handles (no, not love handles) that you can use to select objects and choose a base point for an editing command. Use the DDGRIPS command to turn grips on and to play around with their color and size. Then, when you select an object, all the little handles appear, generally at strategic places such as endpoints and midpoints. Before you get too excited, you should know that the only tasks you can do with grips are stretch, move, copy, rotate, scale, or mirror. You can also change an object's properties.

22 Help!

Here's how to use grips. Select the object, using any selection method. Do *not* start a command. Then click the grip that you want to use as the base point for the operation. It turns red (that's the default) and is now called a hot grip. Right click to choose the operation you want from the cursor menu. If you need to specify a new point (for example, a new location for your grip), do so. In some operations, you can drag the grip. Each operation is slightly different, but the procedure is supposed to be intuitive, so play around. Command line prompts appear, but the point is to manipulate the object using only the mouse. Press Esc once to remove the object from the selection set. Press Esc twice to make the grips disappear.

If the object has an embedded URL, you can also choose Go to URL to launch your web browser and locate the URL.

Help!

Every once in a while, using AutoCAD makes you feel like you've been underwater for too long (you've forgotten to breathe), and you need someone to come rescue you. Sometimes, using Help really helps. Other times, well. . . .

Help comes in two species: regular and context-sensitive. You get to regular help by choosing Help⇨AutoCAD Help Topics. The command teleports you to the Help Contents screen, in which you can choose the topic that you need. If you don't find the contents screen very helpful, click the Index tab. Try typing a topic or key word to see what you get. If you don't get anything, you can scroll through the list and try to find what you want. When you find the topic, double-click it. Sometimes related topics appear in the Topics found box. Double-click again to finally get the help that you want.

Context-sensitive Help displays help on the command that you're using. Start a command and press F1 (or type **'help** in the command line). The Help screen for that command appears. Dialog boxes also contain a Help button that provides Help information for the dialog box. Many dialog boxes have a question mark in the upper-right corner. Click the question mark and click any item on the dialog box to get help related to that item.

Get Me Out of Here!

If you don't want to stay in AutoCAD forever (you could always draw a bed and go to sleep in your drawing), here's how to get out.

Use the QUIT command to exit. An even faster way to quit is to click the Close button (the little x at the top right corner of your screen). Either way, if you haven't saved all your changes, AutoCAD kindly prompts you to do so.

Getting Keen on Release 14

Release 14 has many great new features, most of which are well covered in this book. By skimming for the Release 14 icons, you can easily find them. However, some of these features are not so obvious.

Speed, speed, and more speed

For example, several innovations make Release 14 faster than Release 13:

- ✦ Opening and saving files, redraws and regenerations, and editing operations have been made faster so that you spend less time staring at the screen, waiting.

- ✦ The graphics systems uses less memory which frees up memory for the stuff that counts — faster performance.

- ✦ Zooming and panning in paperspace no longer requires a regeneration each time — less waiting for you.

- ✦ There's a new type of polyline called a lightweight polyline. It works just like the old polyline, but stores vertex data more efficiently. If you have drawings with loads of polylines, you should see smaller drawings and faster regeneration times.

- ✦ Hatches are stored more efficiently in the drawing database. Again, you see smaller drawings and reduced use of memory.

ActiveX Automation: Is it a robot?

No, ActiveX Automation is not a robot. It's Microsoft's facility for customizing applications using VBA — that's Visual Basic for Applications. The great advantage is that it is standard across applications. You can create a macro in Excel using VBA that imports block attribute data from an AutoCAD drawing. The Release 14 support for ActiveX Automation is in the preview stage but Autodesk plans to fully implement it in the future.

Part II

The Commands

Folks, here's the meat and potatoes of the book — a radical statement for a vegetarian like me! Each entry in this part tells you how to execute the command using the menus and the toolbars.

A note about those toolbars. First of all, when you first open AutoCAD, you probably see only four toolbars: the Standard toolbar along the top, the Object Properties toolbar underneath it, and the Draw and Modify toolbars. But AutoCAD has many more toolbars, and you could be a bit mystified when I tell you to use the Solids toolbar and it's nowhere in sight. I humbly refer you to my explanation under the TOOLBAR command in this part, which explains how to pull toolbars out of a top hat. Some toolbars have *flyouts,* which are just visual submenus. You click on a toolbar button, and out flies a bunch more buttons.

Under the "How to Use It" sections that follow each command, I tell you how to use the command, walking you through the prompts or dialog box options. Then you usually find a section called "More Stuff" that includes more advanced or unusual information as well as warnings, tips, and references.

In this part . . .

- ✓ Using commands
- ✓ Finding more information about commands

3D

Draws 3D polygon surfaces.

Toolbar: On the Surfaces toolbar, click the button of the shape you want to draw.

Menu: Choose Draw⇨Surfaces⇨3D Surfaces.

How to Use It

If you use the menu, you get the 3D dialog box. If you use the toolbar, you get a command line prompt. In either case, you have the following options:

 First, specify one corner of the box and then a length and a width. Then type in the height. Specify an angle for the rotation around the Z axis. If you use the Cube option, you only specify the length because the width is the same.

 Instead of using the Box option, you can use the RECTANG command with the Thickness option to create a surface box.

 Specify the center of the base and then specify its radius or diameter. Then type in the radius or diameter of the top. If you type zero, you get a true cone; a bigger number results in a cone with its top chopped off. Now you type in a height and the number of segments, that is, how many facets the cone has.

 A dish is just the bottom half of a sphere. Specify the center, which is the center of the imaginary circle covering the top of the sphere. Then type in a radius or diameter. Now type in the number of longitudinal segments around the sides of the bowl. Then type in the number of latitudinal segments from the bottom of the bowl to its rim.

 This is an upside down dish. It works the same way as the Dish option.

 What is a mesh? You see when you draw one. (I'm so helpful, aren't I?) It's easy. Just specify four corners. Then type in a Mesh M size between 2 and 256, which in AutoCAD jargon, means the number of row vertices, and a similar Mesh N size to specify the number of column vertices.

 This command creates regular and truncated pyramids, ridges (like a pup tent), and tetrahedrons. Specify three base points. You can branch off into tetrahedron making (tetrahedrons have only three base points) and finish it with the apex, or continue bravely on and specify a fourth base point. Now, if you're making a pyramid, all you do is define the apex and you're done. If you want a pup tent, choose the Ridge option and specify the two top ridge points. Finally, if making truncated shapes, choose the Top option and specify three or four top points, depending on the shape. AutoCAD prompts you as you go.

 Specify a center and radius or diameter and type in a number of longitudinal and latitudinal segments as for a Dish.

 This is a 3D donut. Specify the center and then the radius or diameter of the torus. Then define the radius or diameter of the tube, which is the width or fatness of the donut. Finally, type in a number of segments around the tube circumference and around the entire torus circumference.

 This is the shape of a triangular doorstop. It has one right angle. Specify the corner at the right angle, and type in a length, width, and height. Finally, specify a rotation angle about the Z axis.

More Stuff

Because these shapes are surfaces, they can be hidden, shaded or rendered (*see also* HIDE, SHADE, and RENDER).

3DARRAY

Creates 3D arrays.

Menu: Choose Modify⇨3D Operation⇨3D Array.

How to Use It

Before you use this command, be sure that you know how to make plain-Jane 2D arrays. See the ARRAY command.

Select the objects to array. Pick either the Rectangular or Polar option. If you're making a rectangular array, type in the number of rows, columns, and levels (levels is the third dimension). Finally, specify distances between the rows, columns, and levels.

To make a polar array, type in the number of copies you want and the angle to fill, up to 360 degrees. Decide whether you want to rotate objects as they're copied (press **y** or **n**). Now specify a center point for the array. The last prompt is a second point on the axis of rotation. These last two points create an imaginary axis about which the objects are arrayed.

3DFACE

Draws a 3D surface.

Toolbar: Click the 3D Face button on the Surfaces toolbar.

Menu: Choose Draw⇨Surfaces⇨3D Face.

How to Use It

3DFACE creates surfaces in 3D space. You simply specify X,Y,Z coordinates for each point, moving clockwise or counterclockwise. AutoCAD prompts you for the first through fourth points and then continues to prompt you for the third and fourth points so that you can con-tinue to create adjacent faces. Press Enter to end the command.

3DFACE is not an easy way to create surfaces because you have to know the coordinates of each point, but it can be very useful for creating odd-looking surfaces.

More Stuff

Before you specify any point, you can type **i** at the command line to make the edge created by that point and the next point invisible. This process creates realistic-looking models because it creates complex shapes with no internal edge lines.

The EDGE command controls visibility of 3D Face edges. You can also use DDMODIFY edit edge visibility.

3DPOLY

Draws a polyline in 3D space — lines only, no arcs.

Menu: Choose Draw⇨3D Polyline.

How to Use It

AutoCAD starts with the From point: prompt. When you specify the point (using X,Y,Z coordinates), AutoCAD asks you for the endpoint. AutoCAD continues to ask you for the endpoint of segments, and you keep on providing coordinates until you press Enter to complete the command.

The only other options are Undo (for those few of us who may make a mistake specifying those 3D points) and Close, which draws a line from the last endpoint to the first point.

More Stuff

The PEDIT command edits 3D polylines.

ALIGN

Aligns objects with other objects.

Menu: Choose Modify➪3D Operation➪Align.

How to Use It

First, don't let the 3D Operation menu item scare you. Align works nicely for 2D drawing as well. AutoCAD prompts you to select the objects that you want to move. These objects are called *source objects*. You can specify one, two, or three pairs of points.

Aligning using one pair of points is just like using the MOVE command. AutoCAD prompts you for the 1st source point and the 1st destination point. Your first source point may be a corner of the rectangle you want to move. Your first destination point may be the midpoint of a line. The corner of the rectangle moves to the midpoint of the line. When AutoCAD prompts you for the second source point, press Enter to complete the command.

When you use two pairs of points, you can both move and rotate the first object to match the position and angle of the second object. Start in the same way as you do for one-point alignment, but then pick a second source point and a second destination point. Press Enter when prompted for a third source point. AutoCAD asks if you want to scale the object. Choose yes to scale the source object relative to your destination point. AutoCAD moves the first object and rotates it so that the line created by your two source points matches up with the line created by your two destination points.

Using three pairs of points allows a second rotation of the object in a different direction and is used only for 3D objects. Specify three pairs of source and destination points. AutoCAD not only moves and rotates the first object to match up the first two pairs of points but also tumbles the object so that the third pair of points is aligned.

'APERTURE

See also the OSNAP command to do the same thing (that is, change the size of the object snap target box — that's the aperture) using a dialog box.

ARC

Draws an arc.

Toolbar: Click the Arc button on the Draw toolbar.

Menu: Choose Draw⇨Arc.

How to Use It

AutoCAD gives you a dizzying array of options, but the concept is simple. First, choose Start point or Center and specify that point. (You can also press Enter to start your arc at a point that is tangent to the last line or arc you drew.)

AutoCAD then prompts you with your next options and guides you through the creation of your arc. You decide which points you want to specify and in what order. The elements of the arc (depending on your choices) are Start point, End point, Second point, Center, included Angle, Length of chord, and Radius.

More Stuff

See the section "Arcs (the 'erald angels sing . . .)" in Chapter 7 of *AutoCAD Release 14 For Dummies* for more on arcs.

AREA

Calculates area and perimeter of an object or an area you specify.

Toolbar: On the Object Properties toolbar, click Inquiry and then click Area.

Menu: Choose Tools⇨Inquiry⇨Area.

How to Use It

Your options are First point, Object, Add, and Subtract. If you want the area and perimeter of an object, choose Object and then select the object. Select the first point to define an area by selecting points. AutoCAD prompts you for additional points. Add and Subtract enable you to add objects or points until you have the shape you want. Press Enter to complete the command.

ARRAY

Creates copies of an object in a rectangular or polar (that is, circular) pattern.

ATTDISP 31

Toolbar: Click the Array button on the Modify toolbar.

Menu: Choose Modify➪Array.

How to Use It

Select the object or objects you want to copy. Rectangular gives you copies in rows and columns. Tell AutoCAD how many rows and columns you want. Then type in the distance between the rows and columns. (You can also point to diagonal corners of an imaginary rectangle. The rectangle's width and height define the distance between the columns and rows, respectively.) Positive distances build the array up and to the right. Negative distances build it down and to the left.

Select Polar to array copies around a center point. AutoCAD prompts you for the Center point, number of items, and angle to fill (360 degrees fills a circle). You have to specify only two of the three prompts. Press Enter to pass by the prompt you don't want. Finally, tell AutoCAD whether you want to rotate the objects as they're copied.

More Stuff

If you make a mistake, you can wind up with endless copies all over your drawing! Use the U command immediately to undo your array.

ATTACHURL

See INTERNET UTILITIES.

ATTDEF

See the DDATTDEF command.

ATTDISP

Sets the visibility of all attributes in a drawing. An attribute is explanatory text attached to a block.

Menu: Choose View➪Display➪Attribute Display.

How to Use It

When you create an attribute, using DDATTDEF, you decide whether it will be visible or not. This command overrides that

32 ATTEDIT

decision. AutoCAD gives you three options: Normal (does nothing), ON (makes all attributes visible), and OFF (makes all attributes invisible).

More Stuff

Because this command overrides attribute visibility modes, think twice before using it.

ATTEDIT

Changes attribute information and definitions.

Menu: Choose Modify⇨Object⇨Attribute⇨Global.

How to Use It

This command enables you to edit attributes individually, one by one, or to make global changes to all of them at the same time. At the prompt `Edit attributes one at a time? <Y>`, type **y** to be prompted for each attribute individual and **n** to edit globally. Then AutoCAD prompts you for the name of the block, the attribute tag, and the attribute value, so that you can edit all copies of it.

Then you select an attribute and get the following options:

Value	Changes or replaces the value of the attribute. Use Change to change a string of characters instead of replacing the entire value.
Position	Changes the text insertion point.
Height	Changes the text height.
Angle	Changes the rotation angle of the text.
Style	Changes the text style.
Layer	Changes the layer.
Color	Changes the color.

More Stuff

You can use DDEDIT's dialog box to change the attribute's tag, prompt, and default. DDATTDEF creates an attribute.

ATTEXT

See DDATTEXT.

'BASE — 33

ATTREDEF

Redefines a block with attached attributes and updates the attributes according to the new definition.

Command line only

How to Use It

First, explode one copy of the block if you want to change its parts. ATTREDEF prompts you for the name of the block you want to redefine. Then you select the objects for the block, including the attributes. When AutoCAD prompts you for an insertion base point, pick a point. AutoCAD updates the block and its attributes wherever the block has been inserted.

More Stuff

When redefining (or defining) a block, select the attribute text in the same order that you want AutoCAD to prompt you for the attribute information when you insert the block.

AUDIT

Finds errors in the drawing caused by data storage malfunctions.

Menu: Choose File➪Drawing Utilities➪Audit.

How to Use It

AutoCAD asks permission to fix any errors detected. You answer **y** or **n.**

More Stuff

The RECOVER command tries to retrieve those *really* messed up drawings that you can't even open.

'BASE

Sets the insertion base point for your drawing.

Menu: Choose Draw➪Block➪Base.

How to Use It

If you want to change the base point, simply specify the point.

BHATCH

More Stuff

Use this command when you need to insert the drawing into another drawing and want to reference a point on an object. Otherwise, the base point should generally be (0,0,0).

BHATCH

Creates a hatch pattern inside an enclosed area. A hatch pattern isn't an instinct of baby birds. It's just a bunch of parallel lines that fill in an object or enclosed area. This command enables you to create an *associative* hatch pattern; the hatch pattern is adjusted automatically if you change the enclosed area.

With Release 14, you can now use a solid fill to fill in an area.

Toolbar: Click the Hatch button on the Draw toolbar.

Menu: Choose Draw➪Hatch.

How to Use It

The Boundary Hatch dialog box opens; it has four sections:

+ **Pattern Type:** You can use a Predefined hatch pattern — the ones that AutoCAD gives you — a User-defined pattern that creates a hatch out of the current linetype, or a custom hatch pattern that you've created (not ...*For Dummies* material).

+ **Pattern Properties:** Offers the following options:

Pattern	Selects your hatch pattern from AutoCAD's predefined list (or a custom pattern if that's the type you selected).
Scale	Increases or decreases the size of a hatch pattern.
Angle	Rotates the pattern relative to the X axis (but some patterns are created at an angle, so specifying an angle can create unintended results).
Spacing	Defines how wide apart the lines are, only for a user-defined hatch.
Double	Creates a second set of lines 90 degrees from the first set; for user-defined hatches.

+ **Boundary:** You can either pick points or select objects.

+ **Attributes:** You can choose not to create associate hatches or choose to create exploded hatches, in which each line is an individual object.

BLOCK 35

Before you complete the command, click Preview to preview your hatch — a wise idea. The dialog box disappears, and you see what damage you've done. Continue gets you back to the dialog box.

To make things easier, you can specify a hatch you've already created and copy its pattern type and properties to your new hatch. Click Inherit Properties (don't expect to find your rich uncle has left you a major hotel chain), and AutoCAD prompts you to select the original hatch.

After you're all done, click Apply to create the hatch.

More Stuff

Click Advanced, if you're the daring type, for the Advanced Options dialog box. Style defines how objects within objects (islands) are hatched. As you select each type, an image tile shows you an example. Another useful option is Retain Boundaries. If not selected, you get just the hatch without boundaries around it.

See Chapter 12 in *AutoCAD Release 14 For Dummies* for more on hatching.

'BLIPMODE

Turns on and off those pesky little blip marks that appear whenever you pick a point.

Command line only

How to Use It

Type On to show blips; Off if you don't ever want to see them. Blip marks can be useful as reference points.

More Stuff

Even with blipmode on, every time you use REDRAW, REGEN, ZOOM, or PAN, and the drawing is redrawn or regenerated, the blips disappear.

BLOCK

See BMAKE.

BMAKE

Creates one defined object, called a block, from a group of objects, using a dialog box. The block can then be inserted elsewhere using DDINSERT.

 Toolbar: Click the Make Block button on the Draw toolbar.

Menu: Choose Insert↔Block.

How to Use It

Type a name for your block in the Block name box of the Block Definition dialog box. Click Select Objects to return to your drawing and select the objects for the block. Ending object selection returns you to the dialog box. In the Base Point section, click Select Point to pick a base point or type in coordinates. When you insert the block, the base point of the block is placed at the insertion point that you specify in your drawing.

 Use an object snap to create an exact insertion base point. The lower-left corner or center of your block are good choices.

Keep Retain Objects checked to keep the objects you used to create the block. If it isn't checked, your objects disappear when you make the block! Uh oh! Just type OOPS on the command line to bring them back.

More Stuff

Click List Block Names to get a list of all the blocks in your drawing.

 See also DDINSERT, EXPLODE, and WBLOCK for more on blocks. You can also check out Chapter 14 in *AutoCAD Release 14 For Dummies*.

BOUNDARY

Creates a closed region or polyline from objects that form an enclosed area.

Menu: Choose Draw↔Boundary.

How to Use It

The Boundary Creation dialog box appears with the following options:

BOX 37

Object Type	Choose either Region or Polyline.
Define Boundary Set	Leave this option unchecked if you want to do nothing (the easiest option!), and let AutoCAD analyze everything, or check to define a narrower boundary set for quicker results.
Island Detection	Islands are objects inside your objects. Click this option only if you want AutoCAD to pay attention to them.
Pick Points	This option creates the boundary. You pick a point or points inside objects to define the boundary. Press Enter to end the selection of points and complete the command.

More Stuff

See also the PLINE and REGION commands for more information.

BOX

Draws a 3D solid box.

Toolbar: Click the Box button on the Solids toolbar.

Menu: Choose Draw⇨Solids⇨Box.

How to Use It

The first prompt offers you the choice of defining the box from its center or from a corner. If you choose the corner method (the default), specify a point on the bottom of the box. Now you have three options:

Other corner	Specify the diagonally opposite corner of the *bottom* of the box. AutoCAD then prompts you for a height. A positive number makes the box rise along the positive Z axis. (A negative number makes the box descend into — oops — in the direction of the negative Z axis.)
Length	Type **l** and press Enter. AutoCAD prompts you for a length, a width, and then a height. Positive numbers expand the box along positive axes. (Negative numbers expand the box in the direction of the negative Z axis.)
Cube	Type **c** to draw a cube. Of course, all you have to do is specify a length, and AutoCAD figures out that the rest of the sides are the same and draws your cube.

The center option enables you to specify the center of the box instead of the first corner. All the other prompts are the same.

More Stuff

Boxes cannot be stretched or otherwise changed in size. However, you can draw a rectangle and use EXTRUDE to create a solid box.

BREAK

Creates a break in an object.

 Toolbar: Click the Break button on the Modify toolbar.

Menu: Choose Modify⇨Break.

How to Use It

You can do this command in two ways:

1. First, select the object to break by clicking it any old place. Then type **f** (for first point) on the command line and select your first point. Then select your second point. AutoCAD erases the object between the two points. If the second point is beyond the end of your object, AutoCAD erases the object from your first point to its end.

2. If you're the precise type, you can select the object in a location that's also the first point you want to select. Then select the second break point, and you're done.

More Stuff

You can break lines, arcs, polylines, circles, ellipses, donuts, and so on. To break an object into two parts with no gap, type @ for the second point. The object still looks like it's one object but it's actually two.

BROWSER

Opens your Internet browser according to your system's default settings.

 Toolbar: Click the Launch Browser button on the Standard toolbar.

How to Use It

AutoCAD displays the Location <http://www.autodesk.com/acaduser>: prompt. You can press Enter to go to Autodesk's Web site or type in a new location. AutoCAD opens your Web browser

CHAMFER 39

and connects you to the location. Of course, you still have to enter any required passwords and such. By the way, you need either Netscape Navigator 3.0 (or later) or Microsoft Internet Explorer 3.0 (or later) for this command to work.

More Stuff

See also INTERNET UTILITIES for all the Internet commands in one location. Also see DWFOUT which creates files that enable you to display and view AutoCAD drawings on the World Wide Web.

'CAL

An online geometry calculator for evaluating expressions as you draw.

Command line only

How to Use It

This calculator is loaded with features not easily explained in a Quick Reference book. It can calculate regular numeric expressions, as well as work with vectors (lines or any distance and direction), measurements (feet and inches), angles, and more. You can use snap modes in your expressions.

Here are two simple examples:

+ Start the **CAL** command. When AutoCAD prompts you for an expression, type in something like (575+72.2154) * (2^5) − (6 * PI). In other words, something you'd never figure out yourself in a million years. (I got 20692.0, did you?)

+ Say you want to move a circle so that its center is halfway between the midpoint of two lines. Type **move** on the command line and select the circle. When AutoCAD prompts you for a base point, type **cen** and select the circle. At the Second point of displacement prompt, type **'cal** (to use it as a transparent command). AutoCAD asks for an expression. Type **(mid+mid)/2.** AutoCAD then wants to know which midpoints that you're talking about and prompts you to select an object for each midpoint snap. Select one line and then the other. AutoCAD moves the circle. Cool!

CHAMFER

Bevels (cuts at an angle) two intersecting lines (or almost-intersecting lines).

CHANGE

 Toolbar: Click the Chamfer button on the Modify toolbar.

Menu: Choose Modify➪Chamfer.

How to Use It

At the prompt, first define the distances and/or angle. Then repeat the command, select the first line, then the second line, and — presto! — AutoCAD creates a new line at an angle to the original lines. Here are the options:

Polyline	Chamfers an entire polyline (every angle).
Distances	Specifies how far from the second line the chamfer starts.
Angle	Defines the chamfer by a distance from the first line and an angle to the second line.
Trim	Usually, AutoCAD trims the two selected lines so that they meet the chamfer, but you can nix that.
Method	Tells AutoCAD whether to use the Distances or Angle method of defining a chamfer.

More Stuff

You can also chamfer a 3D solid. *See also* the FILLET command.

CHANGE

Changes certain properties of existing objects.

Command line only

How to Use It

First, select the objects.

The first option is Change point. For a line, you pick a new endpoint, and AutoCAD changes the line's endpoint. For more than one line, AutoCAD moves all their endpoints to the change point. For a circle, you specify a point that becomes the new radius. For text, the point you select becomes the new text insertion point. For blocks, the point becomes the new insertion base point. If you select text and press Enter at the Change point: prompt, AutoCAD prompts you to change the text's properties.

The second option is Properties. *See also* the DDCHPROP command.

More Stuff

This command may give you unpredictable results if you select lines with other types of objects, so use CHANGE on one type of object at a time. The DDMODIFY command enables you to change properties of one object.

CHPROP

See the DDCHPROP command.

CIRCLE

Draws a circle.

Toolbar: Click the Circle button on the Draw toolbar.

Menu: Choose Draw⇨Circle.

How to Use It

You have four ways to define a circle:

Center Point	Pick the center point. Then pick a radius or type in a length. Or type **d** (for diameter) and pick the diameter or type in its length.
3P	This isn't the beginning of 3PO's name. (Remember Star Wars?) It stands for 3 point. Specify three points on the circumference of the circle.
2P	You specify two opposing points on the circumference of the circle.
TTR	That means Tangent, Tangent, Radius. You need two other objects nearby for the circle to be tangent to. Select the two objects and then type in a radius length. AutoCAD sometimes gives unexpected results because more than one circle can meet your definition.

More Stuff

See the "(Will he go round in) circles . . ." section in Chapter 7 of *AutoCAD Release 14 For Dummies*.

'COLOR

See the DDCOLOR command.

CONE

Draws a solid cone.

Toolbar: Click the Cone button on the Solids toolbar.

Menu: Choose Draw➪Solids➪Cone.

How to Use It

The default is to create a cone with a circular base. Specify the center point of the base. You can then specify the radius or type **d** to specify the diameter. At the next prompt, type in a height. (A negative height draws an upside-down cone, like an ice cream cone.) Or you can type **a** for apex and specify a point for the apex. Use the apex option if you want a cone that rises at an angle (the Leaning Tower of Pisa look).

If you type **e** for elliptical at the first prompt or use the Elliptical cone button, you define an ellipse just as for the ELLIPSE command, using either the axis or the center method. The rest of the prompts are the same.

More Stuff

See also the ELLIPSE command.

COPY

Copies objects.

Toolbar: Click the Copy button on the Modify toolbar.

Menu: Choose Modify➪Copy.

How to Use It

Select the object or objects that you want to copy and press Enter to complete the selection process.

AutoCAD responds with the Base point or displacement: prompt. To move using the base point method, specify a point as the location to copy from. The point doesn't have to be on the object(s) that you're copying. AutoCAD then prompts you for a second point of displacement that shows the distance and location from the base point. You can pick a point, use an object snap, or type in a coordinate, such as @–2,0.

To move using the displacement method, type the displacement without the @, as in –2,0. At the next prompt, press Enter.

More Stuff

You can type **m** for multiple, and AutoCAD continues to prompt you for second points so that you can make as many copies as you want. Press Enter to complete the command.

CYLINDER

Draws a solid cylinder.

Toolbar: Click the Cylinder button on the Solids toolbar.

Menu: Choose Draw⇨Solids⇨Cylinder.

How to Use It

If you want the base of your cylinder to be a circle, the procedure is quite easy. Choose the Center option and specify the center point of the base circle. Type in the radius or the diameter. Radius is the default, but if you want specify the diameter, type **d.** Now AutoCAD prompts you to type in the height but gives you an option to specify the center of the other end of the cylinder. Either task completes the command.

If you want the base of your cylinder to be an ellipse, choose the Elliptical option. AutoCAD prompts you to define the ellipse. The rest is the same as the circular cylinder, defining either the height or the center of the other end.

More Stuff

You can also draw a circle or ellipse and EXTRUDE it. Also see the ELLIPSE command.

DBLIST

Lists information for every object in the drawing.

Command line only

How to Use It

AutoCAD displays information about every object in the drawing — lots of it. Press Enter to continue from page to page. Press Esc to cancel.

DDATTDEF

Defines an attribute, which is text attached to a block.

Menu: Choose Draw➪Block➪Define Attributes.

How to Use It

Attributes can be used just to facilitate the entry of text labels related to blocks, but they also enable you to extract a database of all the information contained in them. The steps are

1. Create the object. You can make it into a block later.

2. Define the attribute using DDATTDEF. You probably want to put it next to the block. You can define more than one attribute for a block.

3. Back in your drawing, create the block, including in it both the object(s) and the attribute(s).

4. Insert the block. AutoCAD prompts you for the attribute information.

This command opens the Attribute Definition dialog box, which has four sections for you to complete.

Mode:

Invisible	If you click Invisible, the attribute won't show up in your drawing, but you can still extract the information it contains for use in a database.
Constant	You can give an attribute a constant value and then AutoCAD won't prompt you for a value when you insert the block, but just put the constant value in automatically.
Verify	If you click this option, you have to verify that the attribute is correct each time you insert the block. Use this option if you have set a preset.
Preset	Creates a default value that you can change.

Attribute:

Tag	This is the name of the attribute, as in Cost or Manufacturer. Use something meaningful. It can't have any spaces.
Prompt	This is what AutoCAD uses when it prompts you to type in the attribute. It may be the same as the tag or something more helpful. It can have spaces. (But don't get too spacey.)
Value	Use this if you checked Preset to enter the default value.

DDATTE 45

Insertion Point:

You can type in X,Y,Z coordinates or click Pick Point to pick a point in the drawing. As soon as you do, the dialog box magically returns.

Text Options:

Specify the justification, style, height, and rotation of the text as with the text commands.

If you're creating more than one attribute, you can click the Align below previous attribute button to put the attribute directly below the previous one. Click OK to complete the command.

More Stuff

If you make a mistake defining your attribute and catch it before you've defined the block, use DDEDIT. After you insert the block and type in the specific attribute data, use DDATTE to change the data.

See also the DTEXT and STYLE commands for information on setting the text options. ***See also*** the BLOCK and DDINSERT commands for information on creating and inserting blocks.

The ATTDIA system variable determines whether AutoCAD uses a dialog box to prompt you for attribute values when you insert a block with attributes. See Part III. When you use a dialog box, the Verify and Preset modes have no significant meaning.

DDATTE

Edits the data that has been input for the attribute.

Toolbar: Click the Edit Attribute button on the Modify II toolbar.

Menu: Choose Modify⇨Object⇨Attribute⇨Single.

How to Use It

You inserted the block and input the attribute data, but now you need to change the data. Here's how. AutoCAD prompts you to select a block, meaning the one with the attributes you want to edit, and then opens the Edit Attributes dialog box. Just type in the new or corrected data and click OK.

More Stuff

Use DDEDIT to change attribute definitions such as the tag, prompt, and default value. ***See also*** ATTEDIT.

DDATTEXT

Extracts attribute data to a file for use as a database.

Command line only

How to Use It

Now comes the fun stuff, extracting your attribute data into a file for use in a database program. But it ain't easy. Remember, this program is the feared and awesome AutoCAD.

First, you have to make a template file. This is a plain text file that AutoCAD uses to design the database. You can use Notepad which comes with Windows. (Choose Start➪Programs➪Accessories➪Notepad.)

By default, AutoCAD comes with a shortcut to Notepad. Type **Notepad @e**. At the `File to edit:` prompt, press Enter to start a new file and wait until AutoCAD opens Notepad for you.

Say you have a block named DESK. You want to extract the block name, its X and Y coordinates, and two tags: name and phone number. Your kid's teacher may use these attributes to make up a class layout of which student sits where and wants to extract the information to make up a phone tree list of each student's name and phone number.

The attribute file you create in the text editor should look something like the following figure.

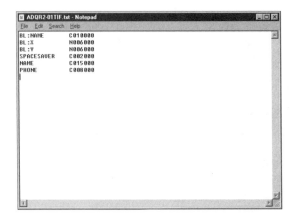

AutoCAD is very finicky about templates. (Oh, for a Template File wizard!) As you type, end each line, including the last, by pressing Enter. Use spaces only, no tabs.

DDATTEXT 47

After you create the template file, save it and remember its name. (Better yet, write it down.) Then go into the DDATTEXT command, which opens up the Attribute Extraction dialog box.

First, select the format you want for the file that you're creating. Usually, you use a comma delimited file, which means that commas appear between the fields of each record, or a space delimited file (you can guess what that means). The fields of space-delimited files have a fixed width. Which to use? That depends on the database application you're going to use. The secret is to go to the documentation of that program and find out what types of files it can import.

Now click Select Objects. This action returns you to your drawing so that you can select the blocks with the attributes that you want in the database. After you're done, the Attribute Extraction dialog box returns.

Next to the Template File button, type in the name of your template file. (You wrote it down, remember?) If you click Template File, you get a dialog box similar to a File⇔Open box that enables you to select the file from a list.

Next to Output File, type a name for the database file you want to create. AutoCAD automatically gives it a *.TXT* file extension. You can also navigate through folders to find the proper location.

Finally, click OK to extract the attribute information and create the database file. Here is the result.

The name of the block (DESK) and the X and Y coordinates are a bit useless, but they're the standard options available with DDATTEXT. (If your kid's teacher needs X,Y coordinates to find your kid, you'd better consider switching schools!)

More Stuff

AutoCAD has several commands (which I left out — they're a book in themselves) that use the AutoCAD SQL Environment (ASE) to help you work with external database management applications.

DDCHPROP

Uses a dialog box to change properties of existing objects: color, layer, linetype, and if appropriate (that means if Ann Landers approves) linetype scale and thickness.

Toolbar: On the Object Properties toolbar, click Change Properties (if you choose more than one object),

Menu: Choose Modify➪Properties (if you choose more than one object).

How to Use It

First, select the objects you want to change.

Color	See the DDCOLOR command.
Layer	See the LAYER command.
Linetype	See the LINETYPE command.
Linetype Scale	See the LTSCALE command.
Thickness	Type the thickness you want.

Click OK to close the Change Properties dialog box.

More Stuff

You can also change the layer of an object by selecting it, clicking the Layer Control drop-down list from the Object Properties toolbar, and choosing a new layer. The Object Properties toolbar also has a Color Control and a Linetype Control drop-down list so that you can change an object's color and linetype.

See the DDMODIFY, DDCOLOR, LAYER, LINETYPE, LTSCALE, and ELEV commands. If you choose only one object, AutoCAD starts the DDMODIFY command, which enables you to change as many properties as that object allows.

DDCOLOR

Sets the color for new objects.

Toolbar: On the Object Properties toolbar, use the Color Control drop-down list and choose a color with no object selected.

Menu: Choose Format➪Color.

How to Use It

This command opens the Select Color dialog box, opening a whole vista of color possibilities. You can select one of the standard colors or select from the full color palette. You can also select BYLAYER, which gives new objects the color assigned to their layer (the default), or BYBLOCK, which draws new objects in the default color until they're grouped into a block. The inserted block takes on the block's color setting.

More Stuff

When you define a layer, you include a color. Generally, the best way to use color is to simply change the layer. Think twice before changing the color of objects using DDCOLOR or COLOR because this change overrides the layer color definition. If objects are on the same layer but have different colors, expect to be confused! See the LAYER command.

DDEDIT

Edits text and attributes.

 Toolbar: Click the Edit Text button on the Modify II toolbar.

Menu: Choose Modify➪Object➪Text.

How to Use It

Select the text to edit. What happens next depends on how you created the text. If you used TEXT or DTEXT, AutoCAD opens the Edit Text dialog box. If you used MTEXT to create paragraph text, AutoCAD opens the Multiline Text Editor. From then on, editing the text is fairly straightforward. Click OK to close the dialog box or text editor and then press Enter to end the command.

The Multiline Text Editor has been enhanced. You can find and replace text, change paragraph properties such as the justification or paragraph width, and change character properties such as font and height.

More Stuff

You can edit attributes with this command, too, but you have to explode the block first. AutoCAD opens the Edit Attribute Definition dialog box, enabling you to change the tag, prompt, and default value.

'DDGRIPS

Turns on grip display.

DDIM

Menu: Choose Tools➪Grips.

How to Use It

The Grips dialog box opens. Click Enable Grips to display them. Click Enable Grips Within Blocks to show grips for each object within the block. If your blocks have many original objects, the number of grips can be a bit overwhelming.

Then choose the color of selected and unselected grips, using the Select Color dialog box. (Refer to the DDCOLOR command.) You also get to choose the size of your grips using the slider bar. To the right makes your muscles bigger; to the left — oh, well.

More Stuff

See Chapters 3 and 7 of *AutoCAD Release 14 For Dummies* for a thorough discussion of grips.

DDIM

Defines dimension settings into dimension styles.

Toolbar: Click the Dimension Style button on the Dimension toolbar.

Menu: Choose Dimension➪Style.

How to Use It

AutoCAD opens the Dimension Styles dialog box, which enables you to control every aspect of the appearance of dimensions. In the Dimension Style section, you can choose the current style from the drop-down list box. To create a new style, define settings using the rest of the dialog box and then type a name in the Name text box. Then click Save to save your style. You can also click Rename to rename a dimension style.

The Family section is where you create families — I'd better be careful what I say here! The default is the Parent — which is the basic style. After you have the default style, you can create variations of the parent — sort of like children, except they have strange names for kids, like Linear, Radial, Diameter, and so on. Unless you're creating a variation of a parent style, leave the Parent button blackened.

Now go on to the three main dialog boxes — Geometry, Format, and Annotation.

Geometry	Make your choices for the dimension line, arrowheads, extension line, and center marks. You also get to choose the scale and whether or not you want to scale to paper space. Click OK.
Format	Here you choose the location of dimension text, arrowheads, leaders, and dimension line. Click OK.
Annotation	Set the definitions for your dimension text and defines the units of measurement. Click OK.

More Stuff

See also all the commands starting with DIM. See the section, "Doing Dimensions with Style(s)," in Chapter 10 of *AutoCAD For Dummies* for the latest and greatest on dimensioning.

DDINSERT

Inserts a block or drawing.

Toolbar: Click the Insert Block button on the Draw toolbar.

Menu: Choose Insert⇨Block.

How to Use It

AutoCAD opens the Insert dialog box. Type in the name of the block or drawing to insert or click Block or File to select from a list. Click Explode if you want the block to be inserted as individual objects.

Click Specify Parameters on Screen if you want to pick the insertion point, scale, and rotation angle on-screen or type your Insertion Point, Scale, and Rotation in the text boxes. Choose OK to insert.

More Stuff

If you click Explode and make a mistake, you may have dozens of itty-bitty objects all over your drawing. You can use U to undo the command, but you can also insert the block unexploded first, to see the results and then explode it.

See also the EXPLODE and XPLODE commands for information on exploding blocks. You find out more in the "Inserting blocks" section in Chapter 14 of *AutoCAD Release 14 For Dummies*.

DDMODIFY

Changes properties of one object at a time.

 Toolbar: On the Object Properties toolbar, click Properties (if you choose one object).

Menu: Choose Modify➪Properties (if you choose one object).

How to Use It

Select the object you want to modify. The dialog box that appears depends on the object you select. Each box has a Properties section enabling you to change color, layer, linetype, linetype scale, and thickness as well as properties that are particular to the object. For example, if you select a circle, you get the Modify Circle dialog box and can change the circles center and radius. The Modify Body dialog box is my favorite — it saves me from having to go to the health spa!

More Stuff

Other related commands: DDCHPROP, DDCOLOR, LAYER, LINETYPE, LTSCALE, and ELEV.

'DDPTYPE

Defines how points are shown.

Menu: Choose Format➪Point Style.

How to Use It

The Point Style dialog box opens. Click on the picture of the style you want. Type in the point size. If you want the points to look the same on your screen no matter how much you zoom in or out, click Set Size Relative to Screen. To see a change in existing points, use REGEN.

DDRENAME

Changes names of objects, like blocks, layers, styles, and views.

Menu: Choose Format➪Rename.

'DDSELECT 53

How to Use It

Select the type of object you want to rename from the Named Objects list. The Items box then lists your objects by name. Select the one you named AuntMelda and type her new name in the Rename To text box. Click OK.

More Stuff

You can't rename certain standard objects such as layer 0, style STANDARD, and so on. You can rename many objects in the same dialog box that creates them. For example, to rename a layer, click Object Properties➪Layers, click the layer name and type the new name.

'DDRMODES

Sets 'ORTHO, SNAP, 'GRID, FILL, 'BLIPMODE, and other drawing aids.

Menu: Choose Tools➪Drawing Aids.

How to Use It

In the Modes section, you turn on or off Ortho, Solid Fill, Quick Text, Blips, highlighting, and groups. Most of these controls are available under their own commands. You can also set how hatches are selected. If you choose the Hatch option, when you select an associative hatch, AutoCAD automatically selects its boundary as well.

The Snap section enables you to turn snap on and off and specify its spacing, angle, and base point. The Grid section enables you to turn the grid on and off and specify its spacing.

The Isometric section turns isometric on and off and sets a plane to the left, top, or right.

On the status bar, you can double-click the SNAP, GRIP, and ORTHO buttons to turn them off and on.

More Stuff

For more information on these drawing aids, see BLIPMODE, FILL, GRID, ISOPLANE, ORTHO, QTEXT, and SNAP. See "Making Your Screen Smart" in Chapter 5 of *AutoCAD Release 14 For Dummies*.

'DDSELECT

Controls how objects are selected.

DDUCS

Menu: Choose Tools➪Selection.

How to Use It

DDSELECT opens the Object Selection Settings dialog box. The Selection Modes section controls the selection of objects.

Noun/Verb Selection	This setting enables you to select objects before starting a command. The cursor includes a pickbox to select objects. You can then give a command that applies to the selected objects. Even with this option on, you can still do it the old-fashioned AutoCAD way — command first.
Use Shift to Add	Requires you to hold down the Shift key to add more objects, as per the Windows custom.
Press and Drag	Requires you to hold down the pick button of your mouse and drag when creating a selection window.
Implied Windowing	The default is on; when you click on an empty spot on your screen, AutoCAD assumes that you want to create a window. If you turn it off, you have to type the w (windows) or c (crossing) option to create a window to select objects.
Object Grouping	You can place objects in named groups.
Associative Hatch	Selecting an associative hatch also selects its boundary.

The next section of the Object Selection Settings dialog box enables you to adjust the Pickbox Size using the slider bar. The Object Sort Method button opens the Object Sort Method dialog box. Object sorting simply forces various procedures (such as object selection by window, object snap, redraws, regens, plotting and Postscript output) to process objects in the order in which you created them.

More Stuff

See the GROUP command for information on creating groups. The SELECT command talks all about selecting objects. See the section "The Selective Service" in Chapter 7 of *AutoCAD Release 14 For Dummies* for a thorough discussion of this command.

DDUCS

Makes a saved UCS current.

 Toolbar: Click the Named UCS button on the UCS toolbar.

Menu: Choose Tools➪UCS➪Named UCS.

How to Use It

AutoCAD opens the UCS Control dialog box, which lists coordinate systems that you've defined. (You define a UCS using the UCS command.) Click the name of the UCS you want and click Current. Then click OK to return to your drawing. You can also delete, list, and rename coordinate systems.

More Stuff

DDUCSP selects one of the coordinate systems that come preset with AutoCAD. That's for the rest of us folks who aren't into making up our own.

DDUCSP

Enables you to change to one of several preset 3D User Coordinate Systems (UCSs).

Toolbar: Click the Preset UCS button on the UCS toolbar.

Menu: Choose Tools⇨UCS⇨Preset UCS.

How to Use It

Click the image tile that shows the view you want. Click OK.

More Stuff

The WCS is the World Coordinate System, which is the default view. The dialog box makes more sense if you click Absolute to WCS, but you can also change the view relative to the current UCS.

The VPOINT and DDVPOINT commands set your viewpoint. The UCS command manages the User Coordinate System which changes the origin and direction of the X and Y axes.

'DDUNITS

Specifies how coordinates and angles are shown, including their precision (the number of places after the decimal point).

Menu: Choose Format⇨Units.

How to Use It

AutoCAD opens the Units Control dialog box. First, select the type of units you want to use. Decimal is the default. Engineering and

56 DDVIEW

Architectural units show feet and inches, using inches for the drawing unit. Otherwise, a unit can be any measurement you want it to be. Then set the precision you want shown.

In the Angles section, you can choose how you want angle degrees shown and their precision.

For more, see the section "Taking Your Measurements" in Chapter 4 of *AutoCAD Release 14 For Dummies*.

DDVIEW

Creates and restores named views.

Toolbar: From the Standard toolbar, on the Viewpoint flyout, click the Named Views button.

Menu: Choose View⇨Named Views.

How to Use It

This command opens the View Control dialog box, which lists the views you've defined and named. A view can be a small, zoomed-in section of your drawing or the whole thing. Naming views helps you get from place to place quickly in a large drawing.

To see a named view, select it from the list, click Restore, and then click OK.

To create a new view, click New to open the Define New View dialog box. Here you name your view (no spaces allowed in the name) and click Current Display (here setting up your display the way you want it before you entered the command helps) or Define Window. Then either type the coordinates of two corners or click Window, which returns you to your drawing momentarily to pick the corners of your view. After you're done, click Save View to return to the previous dialog box.

To delete a named view, select it from the list and click Delete in the View Control dialog box. Try clicking Description to get information describing your view.

More Stuff

Views can be in model or paper space, but you have to be in the same type of space where the view was created to restore it.

DDVPOINT

Controls the 3D angle from which you view your drawing.

Menu: Choose View➪3D Viewpoint➪Select.

How to Use It

AutoCAD opens the Viewpoint Presets dialog box. First, click Absolute to WCS, which calculates relative to plan view and is easiest to comprehend. However, if you like to get esoteric, and are already in some other UCS, go ahead and click Relative to UCS.

If this is your first time using this command, you'll probably have to play around with it and see the results in your drawing before this command becomes clear.

Imagine that you're Superman, flying in around the Earth. In an instant, you can see the Earth from any viewpoint you choose. Now fly back down to Earth and create a viewpoint.

On the left is a square with angles marked about a circle where you define your viewing angle relative to the X axis while remaining in the XY plane (otherwise known as Flatland). Click inside the circle to specify any degree or outside the circle to specify degrees in the increments shown. Or type in the degrees you want in the X Axis text box.

Because zero is the X axis, to the right, if you choose a 45-degree angle, you'll be looking at your 3D object from halfway between its right side and its back side.

Now go to the right side of the dialog box to define your viewing angle relative to the XY plane, which means going up or down in the Z direction. Again you can click on the inside for an exact angle, on the outside for the increments shown, or you can type the degree you want in the XY Plane text box. If you choose a 30-degree angle, you'll be looking at your 3D object from 30 degrees above your object.

Click OK to return to your drawing and see the results. Try DDVPOINT with many different angles until you get the hang of it.

The great thing about this dialog box is the panic button in the middle called Set to Plan View. When you get totally befuddled, click this button to return to 2D space. Ahh, that looks familiar!

More Stuff

VPOINT accomplishes the same thing on the command line using a different system, called the compass-and-axis tripod. You can also

58 DETACHURL

enter X,Y,Z coordinates. See Chapter 15 of *AutoCAD Release 14 For Dummies.*

DETACHURL

See INTERNET UTILITIES.

DIMALIGNED

Draws an aligned linear dimension. When a line is at an angle, an aligned dimension is drawn parallel to the line.

  Toolbar: Click the Aligned Dimension button on the Dimension toolbar.

Menu: Choose Dimension➪Aligned.

How to Use It

You can press Enter and just select an object to dimension. Then AutoCAD automatically creates the extension lines that extend from the object to the dimension line. If you don't like AutoCAD's way of doing things, you can instead pick an origin for the first extension line, and AutoCAD prompts you for the second point.

Next, AutoCAD asks you to specify where you want the dimension line with Text, Mtext, and Angle options. If you specify the location for the dimension command, AutoCAD creates the dimension and ends the command. If you choose an option, AutoCAD prompts you again for the dimension line location, which you specify to complete the command.

Text enables you to customize the text, on the command line. Mtext opens the Multiline Text Editor. In the Text Editor you see brackets which represent the dimension text that AutoCAD thinks you want. You can keep it and add your own text before or after the brackets or delete the brackets and insert your own text.

  When you delete the brackets, you lose *associativity.* That means, if you change the size of the object being dimensioned, the dimension measurement is not automatically adjusted.

Angle changes the angle of the dimension text.

More Stuff

  Remember that the appearance of your dimension is controlled by the DDIM command. Chapter 10 in *AutoCAD Release 14 For Dummies* has more on dimensioning.

DIMANGULAR

Draws an angular dimension that measures an angle.

Toolbar: Click the Angular Dimension button on the Dimension toolbar.

Menu: Choose Dimension⇨Angular.

How to Use It

AutoCAD prompts you to select an arc, a circle, a line, or you can press Return (same as Enter).

If you press Enter, AutoCAD prompts you for three points that define a vertex and two endpoints. This prompt is for measuring an angle that you create "on the fly."

If you select an arc, AutoCAD uses the arc's center as the vertex and measures the angle from the arc's start point to its endpoint.

If you select a circle, you need to tell AutoCAD what part of the circle you want to dimension. The point on which you selected the circle is used as the start of the dimension, so watch where you're pointing! AutoCAD prompts you for a second point. The circle's center is the angle's vertex.

You can even select a line, and AutoCAD asks for a second line that must be at an angle to the first.

After you've finished telling AutoCAD what to dimension, the dimension line location prompt appears with the Mtext/Text/Angle options. If you specify the location for the dimension command, AutoCAD creates the dimension and ends the command.

The Text option enables you to customize the text on the command line. Mtext opens the Multiline Text Editor. In the Text Editor, you see brackets which represent the dimension text that AutoCAD thinks you want. You can keep it and add your own text before or after the brackets or delete the brackets and insert your own text.

When you delete the brackets, you lose *associativity*. That means if you change the size of the object being dimensioned, the dimension measurement is not automatically adjusted.

Angle changes the angle of the dimension text.

More Stuff

Remember that the appearance of your dimension is controlled by the DDIM command. Chapter 10 in *AutoCAD Release 14 For Dummies* has more on dimensioning.

DIMBASELINE

Draws a linear, angular, or ordinate dimension that continues from the beginning of the previous (or a selected) dimension. This means that the second dimension includes the first and the second measurements, the third includes all three measurements, and so on.

Toolbar: Click the Baseline Dimension on the Dimension toolbar.

Menu: Choose Dimension➪Baseline.

How to Use It

If the previous dimension was linear, angular, or ordinate, AutoCAD assumes that you want to continue working from that dimension and enables you to simply specify the beginning of the second dimension's extension line. AutoCAD keeps asking the same question over and over so that you can continue to dimension, until you press Esc.

Or you can press Enter to select a dimension to start from and continue from there. To start from scratch, you first create a regular dimension. Then you can use this command.

More Stuff

Remember that the appearance of your dimension is controlled by the DDIM command. Chapter 10 in *AutoCAD Release 14 For Dummies* has more on dimensioning.

DIMCENTER

Draws a center mark or line through the center of a circle or arc.

Toolbar: From the Dimension toolbar, click the Center Mark button.

Menu: Choose Dimension➪Center Mark.

How to Use It

All you do is select a circle or an arc. That's it. Really.

More Stuff

Use the DDIM command to see the center mark style. Chapter 10 in *AutoCAD Release 14 For Dummies* has more on dimensioning.

DIMCONTINUE

Draws a linear, angular, or ordinate dimension that continues from the end of the previous (or a selected) dimension. Unlike DIMBASELINE, the second dimension does not include the first.

 Toolbar: On the Dimension toolbar, click Continue Dimension.

Menu: Choose Dimension⇨Continue.

How to Use It

First, select the dimension you want to continue next to. Then point to the second extension line or select the object to dimension.

More Stuff

 Remember that the appearance of your dimension is controlled by the DDIM command. Chapter 10 in *AutoCAD Release 14 For Dummies* has more on dimensioning.

DIMDIAMETER

Draws a diameter dimension for a circle or an arc.

 Toolbar: On the Dimension toolbar, click Diameter Dimension.

Menu: Choose Dimension⇨Diameter.

How to Use It

Select an arc or a circle. Move the cursor and watch the dimension move around. Click when you like what you see.

The Text option enables you to customize the text on the command line. Mtext opens the Multiline Text Editor. In the Text Editor, you see brackets that represent the dimension text AutoCAD thinks you want. You can keep it and add your own text before or after the brackets or delete the brackets and insert your own text.

 When you delete the brackets, you lose *associativity*. That means, if you change the size of the object being dimensioned, the dimension measurement is not automatically adjusted.

The Angle option changes the angle of the dimension text.

DIMLINEAR

More Stuff

Remember that the appearance of your dimension is controlled by the DDIM command. Chapter 10 in *AutoCAD Release 14 For Dummies* has more on dimensioning.

DIMEDIT

Edits dimensions. You can change the dimension text as well as its location. You also have an option for creating oblique extension lines, that is, extension lines that come out at some weird angle that happens to suit your needs.

Toolbar: On the Dimension toolbar, click the Dimension Edit button.

Menu: Choose Dimension⇨Oblique — for the Oblique option of DIMEDIT only.

How to Use It

This command provides several options:

Home	Moves the dimension text to its default position.
New	Changes dimension text. AutoCAD displays the Multiline Text Editor, enabling you to edit the text.
Rotate	Rotates the text. You tell AutoCAD the angle.
Oblique	Creates oblique extension lines for linear dimensions. Use this command when the regular extension lines interfere with the rest of your drawing. Type in the final angle you want for the extension lines (not the change from the current angle).

After you've selected your option, AutoCAD prompts you to select objects (you can select more than one dimension). Select the dimension or dimensions you want to change to complete the command.

More Stuff

The DIMTEDIT command moves and rotates dimension text.

DIMLINEAR

Draws linear dimensions.

Toolbar: On the Dimension toolbar, click the Linear Dimension button.

Menu: Choose Dimension⇨Linear.

How to Use It

If you want AutoCAD to automatically create the extension lines, just press Enter and select the object you want to dimension. Otherwise, specify the extension line origins instead.

Then AutoCAD prompts you for the dimension line location with several options.

The Text option enables you to customize the text on the command line. Mtext opens the Multiline Text Editor. In the Text Editor, you see brackets which represent the dimension text that AutoCAD thinks you want. You can keep it and add your own text before or after the brackets or delete the brackets and insert your own text.

When you delete the brackets, you lose *associativity*. That means if you change the size of the object being dimensioned, the dimension measurement is not automatically adjusted.

The Angle option changes the angle of the dimension text.

You can also draw Horizontal, Vertical, and Rotated dimension lines.

More Stuff

Remember that the appearance of your dimension is controlled by the DDIM command. Chapter 10 in *AutoCAD Release 14 For Dummies* has more on dimensioning.

DIMRADIUS

Draws radial dimensions for arcs and circles.

 Toolbar: On the Dimension toolbar, click the Radius Dimension button.

Menu: Choose Dimension⇨Radius.

How to Use It

At the prompt, select an arc or a circle. As you move the cursor, the text moves with it. Click when you like what you see.

The Text option enables you to customize the text on the command line. Mtext opens the Multiline Text Editor. In the Text Editor you see brackets which represent the dimension text that AutoCAD thinks you want. You can keep it and add your own text before or after the brackets or delete the brackets and insert your own text.

DIMSTYLE

When you delete the brackets, you lose *associativity*. That means if you change the size of the object being dimensioned, the dimension measurement is not automatically adjusted.

Angle changes the angle of the dimension text.

More Stuff

Remember that the appearance of your dimension is controlled by the DDIM command. Chapter 10 in *AutoCAD Release 14 For Dummies* has more on dimensioning.

DIMSTYLE

See the DDIM command.

DIMTEDIT

Moves and rotates dimension text.

 Toolbar: On the Dimension toolbar, click Dimension Text Edit.

Menu: Choose Dimension⇨Align Text and then choose an option from the submenu.

How to Use It

AutoCAD prompts you to select a dimension (first if you use the toolbar, last if you use the menu — go figure!). Then you can pick a point for new text location or select one of the options:

Left	Left-justifies the text along the dimension line.
Right	Right-justifies the text along the dimension line.
Home	Returns the text to its default location.
Angle	Changes the angle of the text.
Center	On the menu only, you have a Center option to center the text.

'DIST

Measures the distance between two points.

 Toolbar: On the Inquiry flyout of the Standard toolbar, click the Distance button.

Menu: Choose Tools⇨Inquiry⇨Distance.

How to Use It

Pick two points — AutoCAD tells you the distance between them.

DIVIDE

Divides an object into even segments, placing a point or block of your choice at each division point.

Menu: Choose Draw⇨Point⇨Divide.

How to Use It

Select an object and tell AutoCAD into how many segments you want to divide it.

More Stuff

Use DDPTYPE to control how point objects appear. You may want to choose a more visible point type than usual.

You can select the block option and name a block within your drawing. Choose whether to align the block with the orientation of your object. AutoCAD divides the object using the block instead of points.

DONUT

Draws donuts (or doughnuts if you're hungry), with or without holes.

Menu: Choose Draw⇨Donut.

How to Use It

AutoCAD asks you for inside and outside diameters. If the inside diameter is 0, the donut has no hole. AutoCAD then prompts you for the center of the doughnut (not donut — try it if you don't believe me). Press Enter to end the command or you'll be drawing donuts until the police officers come to eat them up.

More Stuff

The fill mode determines whether your donut is filled in (chocolate) or not (vanilla). See the DDRMODES or FILL commands.

'DRAGMODE

Set the display for dragged objects.

Command line only

How to Use It

Dragging means that when you move or modify an object by dragging, you see a copy of the object that moves as you move your mouse. You have three options:

On	Enables dragging, but you need to type **drag** within the command to see the copy of the object.
Off	Disables the copy completely. You never see it.
Auto	Always shows the copy.

More Stuff

The value of dragmode being on is that you can visualize what your object looks like in its new location or condition. However, dragmode can slow down your system and sometimes is annoying in a complex drawing. So it's up to you.

DRAWORDER

Changes the order in which objects are displayed; especially useful for inserted images and solid-filled objects.

 Toolbar: Click the Draworder button on the Modify II toolbar.

Menu: Choose Tools⇨Display Order.

How to Use It

You have four options:

- ✦ **Send to back** sends the selected objects to the back of the draw order so that anything that can hide it will hide them.

- ✦ **Bring to front** sends the selected objects to the front of the draw order so that they look as if they're on top of everything.

- ✦ **Bring above object** requires you to choose both the objects you want to move above and one reference object. AutoCAD moves the objects above the reference object.

- ✦ **Send under object** requires you to choose both the objects you want to move under and one reference object. AutoCAD moves the objects under the reference object.

More Stuff

If you use the toolbar, the prompts read somewhat differently, but you'll figure it out. If objects don't have some type of fill, you don't see any difference with DRAWORDER. Use it for imported raster images and objects with a fill or hatch.

DSVIEWER

Opens the Aerial View window for quick zooming and panning.

Toolbar: Click the Aerial View button on the Standard toolbar.

Menu: Choose View⇨Aerial View.

How to Use It

AutoCAD opens the Aerial View window with your drawing cozily nestled inside. You do have a menu; however, you can do most of the stuff using the buttons. Before you do anything, make sure that the Aerial View window is active — its title bar should be blue, not gray.

	Pan	Drag the view box to the part of the drawing you want to see. The large-screen drawing pans accordingly.
	Zoom	Click the first corner of the area you want to zoom to, drag to the second corner, and release the mouse button. This area then becomes the new view. The large-screen drawing zooms accordingly.
	Zoom in	This button zooms in on the image only in the Aerial View window.
	Zoom out	This button zooms out on the image only in the Aerial View window.
	Global	This button affects the image only in the Aerial View window, enabling you to see your entire drawing.

More Stuff

Some people like to keep the Aerial View window open a lot for whenever they want to zoom or pan. But AutoCAD then has to update two drawings rather than one, which can slow things down. So deselect Auto Viewport in the Options menu. Then AutoCAD updates the view only when you click on the title bar of the Aerial View window. You can also deselect Dynamic Update in the Options menu so that AutoCAD doesn't update the Aerial View window each time you edit your main drawing.

DTEXT

See also the ZOOM and PAN commands. See "The View from Above: Aerial View" in Chapter 8 of *AutoCAD Release 14 For Dummies*.

DTEXT

Draws text line by line. The D stands for dynamic; you see the text on-screen as you type it in. (That fact may seem mundane to some of you, but us old fogies remember the old days of the plain-Jane TEXT command.)

Menu: Choose Draw⇨Text⇨Single Line Text.

How to Use It

The DTEXT command is suitable for one-line labels.

Pick a start point or provide a justification code or a style. The justification codes offer you many alignment choices for your text. Some of the most useful are

Align	Fits your letters between a start point and endpoint. The size of the letters is adjusted proportionately.
Fit	Fits your letters between a start point and endpoint, but you specify a height, which remains fixed.
Center	Centers the text around a point on the bottom of the letters.
Middle	Centers text both horizontally and vertically around a point.

Some of the others are TL (Top Left), MC (Middle Center), and BR (Bottom Right). You get the idea.

After you decide on your style and justification, pick a start point. If the current text style has no set height, AutoCAD prompts you for a height. Now start typing. Press Enter to end a line. DTEXT continues to prompt you for new text. Press Enter again after the last line to complete the command.

The text you see on-screen moves to its proper justification only after you complete the command.

More Stuff

Use MTEXT for paragraphs. The STYLE command defines text styles. See "Using the Same Old Line" in Chapter 9 of *AutoCAD Release 14 For Dummies*.

DVIEW

Creates parallel projection and perspective views in 3D space.

Menu: Choose View➪3D Dynamic View.

How to Use It

This is a weird one, but here goes. DVIEW is a way of viewing objects in 3D space, using the concept of a camera and a target. You decide where the camera is and what the target is, and AutoCAD shows you what you would see.

The first prompt is to select objects. Select as few as you can for the sake of speed. At the end of the command, you see all the objects that would be seen by the view you've defined. You can also press Enter, and AutoCAD supplies a picture of a darling, little house. You can use the house model to set the angles and distances and then see your picture after you exit DVIEW.

First, type **ca** to place and point your camera. AutoCAD starts you from the center of the drawing. Try moving the cursor to rotate the imaginary camera. First, you're moving up and down, which technically means changing the angle from the XY plane. It's similar to rolling your eyes up and down. Click the Return (right) button of your mouse when you like what you see. An alternative is to type an angle at the command line. An angle of 0 degrees is looking straight out. An angle of 90 degrees looks down from above. The Toggle Angle option toggles between locking the camera at the specified angle and unlocking it so that you can use the mouse to set it.

Now AutoCAD prompts for the angle relative to the X axis. Again you can use the mouse and click the Return button to set the angle, or type in an angle at the command line. In this case, 0 degrees means that you're looking along the X axis toward 0,0. This angle can go from 180 degrees to –180 degrees (both mean the same thing, looking along the X axis out towards infinity — sounds enlightening!).

If you just want a parallel projection view, and you picked only one object, press Enter to see the view. You're done.

If several objects are involved, you can set the target. This action creates your line of sight. Type **ta**. The prompts here are the same as for the camera option. You can press Enter and see a parallel projection view.

The Distance option turns on perspective views (where objects that are farther away look smaller), use the Distance option. A slider bar appears that you can use to set the distance between the camera and your objects. Drag on the slider bar, move your mouse (watch what happens to the slider bar), or type in a number.

The POints option shows you your camera and target points. You can use this option to type in new camera and target (or use object snaps on objects in your drawing).

DVIEW has its own pan and zoom (and so the regular PAN and ZOOM commands can't be used transparently in this command). If you use the OFF option to turn off perspective viewing, zoom moves you in to the center of the drawing, using another slider bar. If perspective viewing is on, zooming in has an effect like going from a wide-angle lens to a normal lens to a telephoto lens.

The CLip option creates invisible walls that obscure what is in front of a front-clipping plane and what is behind a back-clipping plane. Pick either Back or Front and use the slider bar to drag the clipping plane. Or you can pick both Back and Front.

The Hide option removes hidden lines (lines that you wouldn't see from the chosen viewing angle) for the selected objects.

Keep on using options until you're finished defining the view. (There's an Undo option, of course.) Then press Enter to complete the command and see your view.

More Stuff

After you get the view you want, don't expect to ever reproduce it again. So save that view! *See also* DDVIEW.

DWFOUT

Creates DWF (Drawing Web Format) files that you can display and view on the World Wide Web.

Menu: Choose File⇨Export, and then choose Drawing Web Format (*.dwf) from the Save as type drop-down list.

How to Use It

First set up the view of the drawing the way you want it to appear on the Web. For 3D drawings, you may want to use the HIDE command. Saved views are also available so that you can save several views. Paper space is not supported in DWF drawings.

When you use the command, don't forget to choose Drawing Web Format (*.dwf) from the Save as type drop-down list. AutoCAD automatically assigns the file the same name as your drawing, with the *.dwf* extension, but you can change that. Click Save to create the file.

To view the DWF file on the Web, you have to save it to a Web site, using the procedures required by your Internet service provider. Then you need the AutoCAD WHIP! add-on which you can download for free from the Autodesk Web site at www.autodesk.com. You can choose from two flavors of WHIP!, one for Netscape Navigator and one for Microsoft Internet Explorer. So make sure that you download the right flavor. Follow the instructions to install WHIP! Then, when you use your browser to view a page that contains a DWF file, WHIP! automatically kicks in. Right-click on the drawing to open the WHIP! menu. The menu options enables you to pan, zoom, and print.

More Stuff

See INTERNET UTILITIES for a one-stop tour of how to set up URL links in DWF files.

Want to see how WHIP! works but don't have a Web site to upload your DWF drawing to? Your browser can browse DWF drawings on your very own hard drive. It's kind of like surfing in your living room, but — hey! it works. Open your browser, but don't connect to the Internet. In the URL address text box, type the path to your DWF file. Voilà!

DXFIN

Imports a drawing interchange file (DXF). A DXF file is a translation of a drawing into a text file, which is an amazing accomplishment. Because many CAD programs accept DXF files, you use DXF to transfer a drawing from one CAD program to another. (Of course, you'd *never* use any CAD program other than AutoCAD, would you?)

Command line only

How to Use It

First, you must open a spanking clean, new file using the Start from Scratch option in the Create New Drawing dialog box. (This requirement is new for Release 14 and a lot of people are not very happy about it.) AutoCAD opens the Select DXF File dialog box,

DXFOUT

which is like a typical File➪Open dialog box. Browse through drives, directories, and files and then click the file you want. Click Open.

DXFOUT

Creates a DXF file from the current drawing. (See DXFIN for an explanation of DXF files.)

Menu: Choose File➪Export and then select AutoCAD R14 DFX (*.dxf) from the Save As Type drop-down list.

How to Use It

AutoCAD automatically gives the DXF file the current drawing name with a *.dxf* extension. Click Save.

More Stuff

Choose Options where you can

- ✦ Set the accuracy, that is, how many decimal places you want after the decimal point.
- ✦ Click Select objects and make a DXF file from those objects.
- ✦ Choose to make a DXB file, which is a binary file (as opposed to a text, or ASCII, file).

You can also create Release 13 and Release 12 DXF files by choosing them from the Save as type drop-down list.

EDGE

Sets the visibility of 3D Face edges.

 Toolbar: Click the Edge button on the Surfaces toolbar.

Menu: Choose Draw➪Surfaces➪Edge.

How to Use It

EDGE is used only for objects created with 3DFACE. It makes edges visible and invisible, at your command. Select visible edges to make them invisible. To make invisible edges visible, type **d** and then use the All default suboption to display invisible edges with dashed lines. Now you can select them to make them visible. Magic!

More Stuff

See also 3DFACE.

EDGESURF

Draws a 3D polygon mesh surface.

 Toolbar: Click the Edge Surface button on the Surfaces toolbar.

Menu: Choose Draw↷Surfaces↷Edge Surface.

How to Use It

First, you need four touching lines, arcs, or polylines that together create a closed path. To create the surface, all you do is select a point on each of the four edges, in any order. AutoCAD creates a mesh surface.

More Stuff

 The surface created by EDGESURF approximates something that mathematicians call a Coons surface patch. Just think of a small corn patch where raccoons come to feed.

'ELEV

Sets elevation (height above the "ground" XY plane) and thickness of new objects.

Command line only

How to Use It

At the New current elevation prompt, type in a distance, or press Enter if you want to keep the current distance (which is kindly provided to you after the prompt). When AutoCAD prompts for a thickness, type in a number. A circle with a thickness is a cylinder. Objects with thickness are surfaces, not solids.

More Stuff

A negative thickness extrudes objects along the negative Z axis.

ELLIPSE

Draws an ellipse.

 Toolbar: From the Draw toolbar, click the Ellipse button.

Menu: Choose Draw➪Ellipse.

How to Use It

The default is to specify the first endpoint of the first axis. Specify a point. Then specify the other endpoint. AutoCAD asks you for the other axis distance, which is similar to a radius, from the midpoint of the first axis to the edge of the second axis. Specify a point.

You can select Center at the first prompt to draw an ellipse by specifying first its center, the first axis endpoint, and finally the other axis distance.

Select Arc at the first prompt to draw an elliptical arc. Specify the two endpoints of the first axis and the axis distance. AutoCAD goes on to prompt you for a start angle and end angle of the arc. You also have an option to specify the included angle, which is the number of degrees included in the arc starting from the start angle.

More Stuff

See "Ellipses (S. Grant?)" in Chapter 6 of *AutoCAD Release 14 For Dummies.*

ERASE

Erases objects.

 Toolbar: On the Modify toolbar, click the Erase button.

Menu: Choose Modify➪Erase.

How to Use It

It's really simple. Select objects. Press Enter to end the selection process and AutoCAD makes 'em go away.

More Stuff

OOPS restores previously erased objects. U and UNDO undo previous commands and also restore your precious objects.

EXTEND 75

EXPLODE

Breaks up blocks and other compound objects into individual components.

 Toolbar: Click the Explode button on the Modify toolbar.

Menu: Choose Modify➪Explode.

How to Use It

You just select the objects, and AutoCAD explodes them. For example, if you make a block of a square and a circle, you'd have your square and circle back as individual objects.

More Stuff

You can explode not only blocks but polylines, multilines, solids, regions, bodies (sounds messy), and meshes. Also, remember that dimension and hatches are blocks.

 See also the XPLODE command. See the section "Exploding a block" in Chapter 14 of *AutoCAD Release 14 For Dummies* for more.

EXPORT

Translates drawings or objects into other file formats.

Menu: Choose File➪Export.

How to Use It

AutoCAD opens the Export Data dialog box. In the List Files of Type box, choose the format you want to create. In the File Name box, type the name of the file. Click OK. AutoCAD prompts you to select objects. AutoCAD then creates the file.

More Stuff

 AutoCAD has individual commands to export to different formats: DWFOUT, DXFOUT, ACISOUT, 3DSOUT, WMFOUT, BMPOUT, PSOUT, and STLOUT.

EXTEND

Extends a line, arc, polyline, or ray to meet another object.

 Toolbar: Click Extend on the Modify toolbar.

Menu: Choose Modify➪Extend.

76 EXTRUDE

How to Use It

AutoCAD first prompts you for the boundary edges and asks you to select objects. These are the edges you want to extend *to*. Then you select the object you want extended. AutoCAD repeats this second prompt so that you can extend more objects to the original boundary edge or edges. Press Enter to end the command.

More Stuff

If your objects are 3D, this process gets more complicated because what looks like an intersection of objects in 2D may not be in 3D.

EXTRUDE

Creates simple 3D solids by extruding (giving a thickness to) existing, closed, 2D objects.

Toolbar: On the Solids toolbar, click the Extrude button.

Menu: Choose Draw➪Solids➪Extrude.

How to Use It

Select the objects you want to extrude, including closed polylines, circles, polygons, and so on. Don't pick objects that have crossing parts like a figure eight. The default is to then specify a height. If you enter a negative number, AutoCAD extrudes in the direction of the negative Z axis. Now AutoCAD asks for an extrusion taper angle. If you press Enter for the default, which is 0 degrees, you get a solid that rises perpendicular from the original object, with no tapering.

You can specify a taper angle between 0 and 90 degrees to taper in. A taper angle between 0 and –90 degrees tapers out. If the taper angle is too great for the height so that the object would taper to a point before reaching the height you set, AutoCAD refuses to extrude the object.

More Stuff

After selecting your objects, you can select the Path option. You select an object to be the path. It can be curved. The path object cannot be in the same plane as the 2D object you're extruding. See the "Extruding" section in Chapter 15 of *AutoCAD Release 14 For Dummies* by Bud Smith.

'FILL

Sets the fill mode for multilines, solids, solid-filled hatches, and wide polylines.

Command line only

How to Use It

You have two choices. On means fillable objects are filled. Off means objects aren't filled.

More Stuff

Lots of filled objects in your drawing slows down regeneration time. You can turn fill mode off until you've finished your drawing. Actually, printing or plotting filled objects takes a while and certainly takes more ink! You also can set the fill mode using DDRMODES.

FILLET

Rounds off (fillets) the edges of objects to make rounded corners.

Toolbar: Click the Fillet button on the Modify toolbar.

Menu: Choose Modify⇨Fillet.

How to Use It

The simple way to use this command is to select your first object at the prompt and then select the second object. AutoCAD fillets them. AutoCAD extends or trims your objects as necessary. If one of your objects is an arc or a circle, more than one possible way to fillet may exist. AutoCAD creates a fillet with endpoints closest to the points you used to select the objects.

If you choose the Polyline option and select a polyline, AutoCAD fillets the polyline at every possible vertex.

Choose the Radius option to specify the radius of future fillets. For some reason, this option ends the command, so use it again if you actually want to fillet something with the new radius.

You have a Trim option. Usually, AutoCAD trims your lines to make a neat fillet, but if you choose No Trim, AutoCAD makes the fillet and leaves the lines, too. A little messy, if you ask me.

'FILTER

More Stuff

You can also fillet 3D solid objects. If you select a 3D solid object, AutoCAD prompts you accordingly.

'FILTER

Creates a filtered list of objects to help you select objects based on their properties.

Command line only

How to Use It

You can create a filter first and then use it on an editing command using the Previous option. Generally, you use a filter transparently, within a command. Start the command and, at the Select objects prompt, type **'filter**.

AutoCAD opens the Object Selection Filters dialog box. The top shows your current filter lists. Use the Select Filter section to create new filters. Follow these steps:

1. Pick an item from the drop-down list. If the item is an object such as a circle, you can go directly to Step 5. AutoCAD creates the filter Object = Circle.

2. If appropriate, add an operator from the table below. For example, if you choose Circle Radius, you need to add an operator and a value.

3. If the item has a limited number of values, choose Select and choose the value from the drop-down list. For example, you can choose the name of a layer from the list.

4. If you want to assign a value, type the value next to the X text box. For example, if you choose Circle Radius and the operator is = (equals) you can type 3 to select circles whose radius equals 3.

5. Choose Add to List.

6. Continue to add filter statements to your heart's desire. You can add logical operators (AND, OR, and so on) around them. The logical operators are at the end of the drop-down list of items. Logical operators must be paired before and after the objects they apply to.

7. After you've completed your filtering statements, type a name for your filter next to the Save As box and click Save As. It always pays to save!

8. Click Apply.

9. In your drawing, AutoCAD prompts you to select objects. You thought you just did that! Type **all** or make a window around all the objects you want to apply the filter to. Press Enter to end object selection and presto! Only the objects that satisfy your filter make it through.

10. Now go do something with those objects.

You can use the following operators to define the filter.

Operator	Meaning
=	Equals
!=	Not equal to
>	Greater than
>=	Greater than or equal to
<	Less than
<=	Less than or equal to
*	Equal to any value

'GRID

Displays a grid of itsy-bitsy, teeny-weeny gray polka-dots.

Command line only

How to Use It

AutoCAD gives you the following options:

Grid spacing(x)	Type a number to specify the spacing of the grid dots in units. Type a number followed by **x** to set the grid equal to that number times the snap interval.
ON	Turns on the grid.
OFF	Turns off the grid. (Did you guess?)
Snap	Sets the grid spacing equal to the snap interval.
Aspect	This option is used to set the X spacing and Y spacing to different numbers.

More Stuff

The grid is used to get your bearings. It's useful to set the grid to the snap setting so that you can see where the snap points are. On the other hand, having all those dots on your drawing can be very annoying. If you don't like the grid, you don't have to grid and bear it — turn it off.

See also the SNAP and DDRMODES commands.

GROUP

Creates a named group of objects.

Menu: Choose Tools⇨Object Group.

How to Use It

AutoCAD opens the Object Grouping dialog box. On top is a list of existing groups.

To create a group, type a name in the Group Name text box. You can provide a description of it in the Description text box if you want. In the Create Group section, click Selectable. This option means that when you select one object in the group, you get 'em all, which is the point of creating a group. (But you may want to turn off the Selectable feature, if you need to work with only one object in the group.)

Then click New to create the group. AutoCAD returns you to your drawing. Select the objects for your group and press Enter to complete the selection process. Back at the ranch (the Object Grouping dialog box), y'all click OK to complete the command.

Using the group when you select objects is automatic. Select one object, and they all come along.

You can type the group name at the Select objects prompt to select the group.

More Stuff

The Change Group section enables you to edit groups. You can remove objects from and add them to the group, change the group's selectable status, or rename it.

HATCH

See the BHATCH command to create hatch patterns using a dialog box.

HATCHEDIT

Edits a hatch.

 Toolbar: Click the Edit Hatch button on the Modify II toolbar.

Menu: Choose Modify➪Object➪Hatch.

How to Use It

AutoCAD prompts you to select a hatch object. When you do, the Hatchedit dialog box opens, which is the same as the Boundary Hatch dialog box you get with the BHATCH command. Make the changes that you want and click Apply.

See the BHATCH command for details on using the dialog box.

HIDE

Hides lines of a 3D surface or solid object that would naturally be hidden from the 3D view you're using.

 Toolbar: Click the Hide button on the Render toolbar.

Menu: Choose View➪Hide.

How to Use It

Before using this command, you need a 3D object. And you need to use VPOINT or DVIEW to create a 3D view of your object. When you choose this command, AutoCAD goes ahead and hides lines that are at the back of your object.

More Stuff

HIDE doesn't hide objects on layers that are frozen or turned off.

'ID

Gives you the coordinates of a selected point.

 Toolbar: On the Standard toolbar, from the Inquiry flyout, click the Locate Point button.

Menu: Choose Tools➪Inquiry➪ID Point.

How to Use It

Just pick a point. Using an object snap is a good idea. AutoCAD lists the point's coordinates.

IMAGE & IMAGEATTACH

Inserts raster (bitmap) images into your drawings.

Toolbar: Click the Image button on the Reference toolbar.

Menu: Choose Insert⇨Raster Image.

How to Use It

IMAGE opens the Image dialog box where you can control images in your drawing. From here you can attach, detach, reload, and unload images. Images are generally bitmaps, which means they're made up of little dots (bits). Click Attach to attach an image using the Attach Image dialog box. (The IMAGEATTACH command opens this dialog box immediately for you.) Type the image file name or click Browse to navigate to it. Check the Specify on-screen boxes to get prompts for the insertion point, scale factor, and rotation angle. Click OK to insert the image.

More Stuff

You can insert BMP, TIF, RLE, JPG, GIF, and TGA files. Click Details in the Attach Image dialog box to get resolution and size information about an image.

IMAGEADJUST

Controls brightness, contrast, and fade of an image.

Toolbar: Click the Image Adjust button on the Reference toolbar.

Menu: Choose Modify⇨Object⇨Image⇨Adjust.

How to Use It

Select an image. Use the slider bars to adjust the brightness, contrast, and fade. The preview box enables you to see the result. Click Reset to return to the original settings.

IMAGECLIP

Displays only the portion of an image inside a boundary you specify.

Toolbar: Click the Image Clip button on the Reference toolbar.

Menu: Choose Modify⇨Object⇨Image Clip.

How to Use It

At the `OFF / ON / Delete / <New Boundary>` : prompt, type **off** to turn off an existing boundary, **on** to turn on an existing boundary that you had turned off, or **d** to delete an existing boundary. To create a new boundary, press Enter. You then have a choice of creating a polygonal or a rectangular boundary. Press Enter to create a rectangular boundary and pick two corners of the rectangle. Type **p** to create a polygonal boundary and pick all the points that you want to create the boundary. Press Enter to complete the boundary. AutoCAD displays only the portion of the image inside the boundary.

IMAGEFRAME

Turns image frames on and off.

Toolbar: Click the Image Frame button on the Reference toolbar.

Menu: Choose Modify⇨Object⇨Image⇨Frame.

How to Use It

By default, images have a frame. You can turn off (type **off**) the frames of all the images in your drawing, if you don't like the way they look. Problem is, after turning off the frame, you can't select the images! So turn them back on, of course (type **on**).

IMAGEQUALITY

Enables you to display an image at high or draft quality.

Toolbar: Click the Image Quality button on the Reference toolbar.

Menu: Choose Modify⇨Object⇨Image⇨Quality.

How to Use It

This command has two options, High and Draft. Pick one.

IMPORT

Translates other file formats into AutoCAD drawings.

Toolbar: Click the Import button on the Insert toolbar.

How to Use It

AutoCAD opens the Import File dialog box. In the List Files of Type list box, select the format type of the file that you want to import. Select the filename from the File Name list box.

More Stuff

Also, you have individual commands for specific formats: the 3DSIN, DXFIN, DXBIN, ACISIN, WMFIN, and PSIN commands. For bitmap files, use IMAGE.

INETCFG

See INTERNET UTILITIES.

INSERT

See DDINSERT, which does the same thing but uses a dialog box.

INSERTURL

See INTERNET UTILITIES.

INTERFERE

Creates a solid object from the volume where two or more solids overlap.

 Toolbar: Click the Interfere button on the Solids toolbar.

Menu: Choose Draw⇔Solids⇔Interference.

How to Use It

AutoCAD prompts you for the first set of solids (after which you press Enter) and then for the second set of solids. Usually, you're just selecting one solid for each set, but you can pick any number. AutoCAD checks the first set against the second set for overlapping. When you're finished selecting, press Enter and watch AutoCAD figure it out. AutoCAD asks you whether it should create the interference solids. Type **y** to create them.

If there is more than one pair of interfering solids, the next prompt begs your permission to highlight pairs of interfering solids. The idea here is that if you've selected lots of solids, the different interfering pairs may be hard to distinguish.

INTERNET UTILITIES

(I know — we can call them in-laws!) AutoCAD offers you the opportunity to see the next pair highlighted. Type **x** to end the command.

INTERNET UTILITIES

A group of commands for preparing drawings to display on the Internet.

Toolbar: On the Internet Utilities toolbar, choose one of these buttons: Attach URL, Detach URLs, List URLs, Select URLs, Open from URL, Insert from URL, Save to URL, Configure Internet Host, Internet Help.

How to Use It

First, you need to know how to find the Internet Utilities toolbar. Right-click any toolbar. In the Menu Group drop-down list, choose `inet` (for Internet Utilities). Now check Internet Utilities from the Toolbars listing. See "More Stuff" below if `inet` isn't listed.

You use the URL commands before you create the DWF file from your drawing.

- ✦ **Attach URL:** Enables you to create a link between a web address (URL) and an area or object in your drawing. Type **a** to link to an area and **o** to link to one or more objects. Then AutoCAD prompts you for the URL which you need to type.

- ✦ **Detach URL:** Detaches URLs from objects or area. Pick the objects or select the area (AutoCAD creates a rectangle for area URLs.) Save the drawing before making the DWF.

- ✦ **List URLs:** Lists the URLs attached to selected object. Select the objects to get the list.

- ✦ **Select URLs:** Selects all objects in a drawing that have attached URLs. You can then use List URLs to get a list of all the URLs in a drawing.

- ✦ **Open from URL:** Enables you to open a drawing from a URL you specify on the Internet, your intranet, your network, or your computer. If you specify a URL on the Internet, you must be connected to the Internet first.

- ✦ **Insert from URL:** Enables you to insert a drawing from a URL. It works like OPENURL but the drawing is inserted in your current drawing.

INTERSECT

Cool tip! If you're viewing a DWF drawing on the Internet and the actual DWG drawing is in the same folder as the DWF folder, you can open or insert the drawing using drag-and-drop. To open the drawing, hold down Ctrl and Shift and drag the DWF image. Release the mouse when the image is in your AutoCAD drawing area and then release the Ctrl and Shift buttons. To insert the drawing, just hold down Ctrl.

✦ **Save to URL:** Saves your drawing to the Internet. You specify the URL in the following format:

ftp://servername/pathname/filename.dwg

✦ **Configure Internet Host:** Enables you to configure how AutoCAD accesses the Internet for you. AutoCAD's default settings may work for you; otherwise, ask your system/web site administrator. You can set passwords and login names if needed.

✦ **Internet Help:** Opens the special help file for the Internet Utilities.

More Stuff

If `inet` is not listed in your Menu Group listing, you need to load the menu. Here's how. From the menu choose Tools➪Customize Menus. Click Browse. AutoCAD shows you the \support folder. Choose `inet.mnc` and click Open. In the Menu Customization dialog box, click Load. Close the dialog box. Now open the toolbar as I explain in the "How to Use It" section.

See also the DWFOUT and BROWSER commands.

INTERSECT

Creates a region or solid from the overlapping area or volume of two or more regions or solids.

Toolbar: Click the Intersect button on the Modify II toolbar.

Menu: Choose Modify➪Boolean➪Intersect.

How to Use It

First, select either regions (2D) or solids (3D). AutoCAD does the rest. What you're left with is only the area or volume that was in common among the selected objects. The rest goes bye-bye.

'LAYER 87

'ISOPLANE

Selects an isometric plane.

Command line only

How to Use It

The default at the prompt is a toggle that rotates planes from left to top to right. You can also simply choose Left, Top, or Right. SNAP must be on and set to isometric.

After you're in isometric mode, forget this command. Use F5 instead to move from plane to plane. (Don't forget your parachute!)

More Stuff

You use the DDRMODES command to turn isometric planes on and off.

'LAYER

Everything you ever wanted to know about layers.

Toolbar: Click the Layers button on the Object Properties toolbar.

Menu: Choose Format⇨Layer.

How to Use It

The Layer Control dialog box gives you full control over — you guessed it — layers. At the top, the current layer appears. To create a new layer, click New. AutoCAD names the new layer with a creative name such as Layer1, but highlights it so that you can immediately rename it. Press Enter to lock in the name. (Names can be up to 31 characters long — no spaces allowed.) By default, AutoCAD makes your new layer black with a continuous linetype. To dress things up a bit, do the following:

✦ Click the color box to open the Select Color dialog box and choose a color.

✦ Click the linetype to open the Select Linetype dialog box and choose a linetype.

Linetypes have to be loaded the first time you use them. Click Load.

Choose Current if you want your new layer to be the current layer.

88 LEADER

You can do three things to layers:

Turn Off and On	On is the normal state for a layer. If you turn it off, the layer becomes invisible, but still regenerates when the drawing regenerates.
Freeze and Thaw	Thawed is the normal state for a layer. If you freeze it, the layer becomes invisible and is not regenerated. You can also freeze and thaw layers in current or new floating viewports, if you're working in paper space.
Lock and Unlock	If you lock a layer, it's visible but cannot be edited. This can make editing overlapping objects on other, unlocked layers easier.

To change a layer's status, find the column that you want and click the icon. The columns are so tiny that you can't see their heading names. If you hold the mouse cursor over a column, the column's name appears as a ToolTip. You can also drag the columns at their heading to change their width.

You can select more than one layer at a time by pressing Ctrl as you click. To select a range of layers, hold down Shift and click the first and last layer you want to choose. Select a layer name again to deselect it. Another trick is to right-click in the Name list area and choose Select All or Clear All from the menu that pops up.

To delete a layer, choose it and click Delete.

More Stuff

Freezing layers, or turning them off, is very useful in a complex drawing. However, forgetting what you can't see is all too easy!

Other related commands are DDCOLOR, LINETYPE, PSPACE, and VPORT.

The easiest way to make a layer current is to use the Layer Control drop-down list on the Object Properties toolbar. Just pick the layer you want — but make sure that no object is selected or else you change the object's layer! See "Getting the layered look" in Chapter 3 and "Using that layered look" in Chapter 5 of *AutoCAD Release 14 For Dummies*.

LEADER

Creates a line used to connect annotation text with its object. The leader usually has an arrow pointing to the object.

Toolbar: Click the Leader button on the Dimension toolbar.

Menu: Choose Dimension⇨Leader.

How to Use It

AutoCAD prompts you for the start point, which is often at the object that you want to annotate. Then AutoCAD keeps on prompting you for points. After you're finished drawing lines, press Enter, and AutoCAD prompts you for an Annotation. If you just want one line of text, press Enter and type it at the command line. Press Enter to ignore the Mtext prompt and complete the command.

If you select Format at the first prompt, you can choose to draw the leader as a spline or choose other format options. Then specify the endpoint of your leader and press Enter at the prompt to get other options:

Mtext	Press Enter and specify two points that define the boundary of the text. Specify the height and rotation angle of the text boundary. AutoCAD then opens the Edit Mtext dialog box, and you type in your text. Click OK to complete the command.
Tolerance	Enables you to create a feature control frame with geometric tolerances. If you don't know what that is, you probably don't want to do this option. But if you're interested, see the TOLERANCE command for details.
Copy	Copies an object and attaches it to the end of the leader. You get to select the object.
Block	Inserts a block at the end of the leader line, prompting you for an insertion point, scale, and rotation angle.
None	Use this option if you don't want to add any text to the leader.

More Stuff

Leader styles are controlled through the DDIM command.

LENGTHEN

Lengthens lines, arcs, open polylines, elliptical arcs, and open splines. Also changes the angle of arcs.

 Toolbar: Click the Lengthen button on the Modify toolbar.

Menu: Choose Modify⇨Lengthen.

How to Use It

Select an object. AutoCAD lengthens a line from the endpoint closest to your selection point.

LIGHT

You have four ways to lengthen a line:

Delta	Specify the increase in length. Or, if you select the angle option, specify the increase in the angle.
Percent	Specify the increased length as a percentage of its current size. 100 means no change. Type 200 if you want to double the length of the object.
Total	Here you specify the total length (or included angle).
Dynamic	AutoCAD enters Dynamic Dragging mode, enabling you to drag the object to the desired length (or angle).

AutoCAD prompts you to select an object. You may reason that you've already done that, but you have to select it again to lengthen it. AutoCAD prompts you for more objects to lengthen (as if you have nothing else to do). Press Enter to get on to better things. The Undo option enables you to undo the last lengthen.

LIGHT

Creates lights for use in a rendered scene.

Toolbar: Click the Lights button on the Render toolbar.

Menu: Choose View⇨Render⇨Light.

How to Use It

This command opens the Lights dialog box. In the Lights list box is a list of all lights that you've already defined. Select a light and click the Modify button to modify a light. Modifying a light uses the same dialog box as creating a new one, so refer to the next few paragraphs. Select a light and click the Delete button to delete a light. Click the Select button to return to your drawing so that you can select a light by clicking it. That's if you know where it is but forgot its name.

On the right side of the dialog box is the Ambient Light section. Ambient light is background, overall light that covers all the surfaces in your drawing. Use the slider bar to adjust the Intensity, or type in a number from 0 (no light) to 1 (full brightness). Too low a number can make your drawing appear like a dark room (or a romantic night scene). Too high a number can make your drawing look like an over-exposed photograph. Try starting with 0.3.

In the Color section, choose the ambient's light color. You can use the Red, Green, and Blue slider bars, or click Select Custom Color. Maximum red, green, and blue produce white light. (Light colors don't mix like paint colors.)

LIGHT 91

Now create some lights. (Makes you feel all-powerful, doesn't it?) Next to the New button is a drop-down list of three types of light. Select one of them and click New to create a new light of that type.

Point Light

Choosing Point Light opens the New Point Light dialog box. A point light is like a light bulb. It emits light that radiates out in all directions, and it attenuates, which means the light gets fainter as it gets farther from its source. First, type a name for your light in the Light Name text box (you can use up to eight characters). If you're creating different kinds of lights, it's a good idea to give the lights names that tell you what kind of light it is. For example, PL1 for the first point light. (I'm sure that you can be more creative than that, but you get the idea.)

Next, set the Attenuation (that's how a light fades with distance). You can choose None, Inverse Linear, or Inverse Square. When selecting attenuation, remember that the brightness of inverse square drops off much more quickly than that of inverse linear.

Now set the Intensity of the light, using the slider bar or the text box. It can be any real number. However, the default is based on the attenuation setting. Defaults are usually good settings to start with and then you can experiment.

The following table displays the default intensity setting that corresponds with each attenuation setting.

Attenuation Setting	Default Intensity
None	1
Inverse Linear	One-half the extents distance from the lower-left to the upper-right corner
Inverse Square	One-half the square of the extents distance from the lower-left to the upper-right corner

So if you've chosen inverse linear attenuation, and your drawing extends from 0,0 to 120,90, the extents distance is 150, and the default intensity is 75.

To set the position of your light, click the Show button to see the current location. AutoCAD automatically places the light at the center of the current viewport. (Point lights radiate light equally in all directions, so there is no target.) You may want to write down the location coordinates. Click OK. Now click Modify. This action returns you to your drawing. AutoCAD has placed a point light block in your drawing so that you can see where it is. You can pick a point or type in coordinates. However, don't forget that you usually don't want your light to be "on the ground." You want to include a Z coordinate.

Finally, select the light's color. This selection works just like the setting for Ambient Light in the Lights dialog box, discussed previously in this section. Check Shadows On if you want to create shadows. Click OK, and you return to the Lights dialog box.

Distant Light

Choose Distant Light from the drop-down box in the Lights dialog box and click New to get to the New Distant Light dialog box. A distant light produces parallel light beams in one direction and does not attenuate. This light is supposed to be sort of like the sun. (You *are* getting all-powerful here, aren't you?) Type in a name for your distant light in the Name text box. The intensity can range from 0 (off) to 1 (full intensity). The color is set in the same way as for Ambient Light in the Lights dialog box, explained earlier.

You can set the location of a distant light by using the astronomical terms *azimuth* and *altitude,* or by using the Light Source Vector system. Azimuth means the degrees from North. You can go from −180 to 180, both of which are south. Altitude goes from 0 (ground level) to 90 (straight overhead). Actually, in the text box, you can type a number between 0 and −90. You can also use the slider bar. The results of this process are shown in the Light Source Vector section, which defines the light source using X,Y,Z coordinates. Conversely, if you type coordinates in the Light Source Vector section, the Azimuth and Altitude numbers change accordingly.

All these steps are supposed to create a direction for your distant light. If you want, you can create a direction by clicking Modify in the Light Source Vector section. AutoCAD returns you to your drawing and prompts you for a light direction to and a light direction from. You can pick points, but typing them in is more accurate. Remember that the sun usually comes from above the horizon, so you want to pay attention to the Z coordinate. (You don't want to totally change the laws of nature.)

For ultra-realism, click Sun Angle Calculator, which calculates the location of the distant light based on latitude, longitude, and time of day. If you don't know the latitude and longitude, click Geographic Location where you can pick from a list of major cities from around the world or click a location on a map. It's a great way to travel without leaving your chair!

After you're done, click OK until you return to the Lights dialog box. Click North Location. The default is the positive Y axis direction but you can change that to any direction you want.

Spotlight

Choose Spotlight from the drop-down list in the Lights dialog box, click New, and you're ready to create a new spotlight. A spotlight produces light in a cone shape, radiating in a specific direction. The New Spotlight dialog box is very similar to the New Point Light dialog box, discussed earlier in this section. Here are the features that differ:

Position	You need not only a location but also a target.
Hotspot and Falloff	Spotlights have a hotspot, that is, the brightest cone of light. The default is 44 degrees. Falloff is the widest cone of light. The default is 45 degrees. Both can range from 0 to 160 degrees. If the hotspot and falloff angles are the same, the whole cone is bright. If the falloff is a few degrees larger than the hotspot, the result is an area of softer light around the edge of the spotlight. You can get some cool effects this way.

Because spotlights have a location and a target, attenuation is calculated from the location to the object, rather than to the drawing's extents.

More Stuff

Use your lights with the SCENE and RENDER commands.

'LIMITS

Sets drawing boundaries.

Menu: Choose Format⇔Drawing Limits.

How to Use It

To specify the limits with X,Y coordinates, AutoCAD prompts you first for the lower-left corner. These coordinates are usually **0,0**. Then type in coordinates for the upper-right corner.

You can also turn limits checking on. AutoCAD rejects points entered outside the limits. If you feel too rejected, you can turn limits checking off, too.

More Stuff

AutoCAD uses the limits when you use the ZOOM command with the All option. Also, when you turn on the grid, AutoCAD uses the limits for the grid boundaries. For more on limits, see the "Set Some Limits!" section in Chapter 4 of *AutoCAD Release 14 For Dummies*.

LINE

Draws lines.

Toolbar: Click the Line button on the Draw toolbar.

Menu: Choose Draw⇨Line.

How to Use It

LINE is surely the most commonly used command in AutoCAD. And it's easy! AutoCAD prompts From point:, and you specify the start of your line. AutoCAD then prompts To point:, and you specify the endpoint of your line. Often, you want to continue drawing connected lines, so AutoCAD continues to prompt you for points, and you continue to specify endpoints of new lines until you press Enter to end the command.

At any time, you can type **u** and press Enter to undo your last line segment. Also, if you've drawn more than one line, you can type **c** and AutoCAD closes your lines — that is, draws a line from the endpoint of your last line to the beginning of your first line.

If you end the command and then decide you want to continue drawing lines from the end of the last line (or last arc), press Enter at the From point: prompt, and AutoCAD pick ups where you left off.

More Stuff

PLINE creates 2D polylines that can have width and can be filled. RAY creates a line that starts but *never* ends. (I just say that to get you interested. But go look it up, and you'll see that I'm right.) XLINE creates a line that never starts or ends but exists nevertheless (it's a riddle). MLINE creates multiple, parallel lines. See "Lines (lines, everywhere a line . . .)" in Chapter 6 of *AutoCAD Release 14 For Dummies*.

'LINETYPE

Sets current linetype, loads new ones, and sets linetype scale.

Toolbar: Click the Linetype button on the Object Properties toolbar.

Menu: Choose Format⇨Linetype.

How to Use It

The Layer & Linetype Properties dialog box pops open, Linetype tab on top, with a list of loaded linetypes. Select one and choose OK to make it current.

You can also specify an ISO pen width and linetype scale.

If you click Load, you go to the Load or Reload Linetypes dialog box. The default file, acad.lin, has the standard linetypes, but you can load another file (with filename extension .lin) that you've created. You can then select any or all linetypes to load and use in your drawing. Click OK to return to the Select Linetype dialog box. Then select a linetype from the Loaded Linetypes list and click OK.

More Stuff

When you define a layer, you include a linetype. Generally, the best way to use a new linetype is to simply change the layer. Think twice before changing the linetype of objects because this change overrides the layer linetype definition. See the LAYER command for information on creating layers.

LIST

Lists database information for the object or objects you select. This list includes everything that you ever wanted to know about the object and more, including its coordinates, size, layer, and type.

 Toolbar: On the Inquiry flyout of the Standard toolbar, click the List button.

Menu: Choose Tools➪Inquiry➪List.

How to Use It

I love this command. To find out all about the objects you've drawn is so satisfying. All you do is select objects, and AutoCAD tells all.

More Stuff

 You may need to switch to the text screen to see everything AutoCAD has spit out about your object. Press F2. Use F2 again to get back to your drawing.

LISTURL

See INTERNET UTILITIES.

LOGFILEOFF

Stops recording the text window contents and closes the log file.

Command line only

How to Use It

I explain how to use the log file under LOGFILEON. You can also use the PREFERENCES command, under the General tab.

LOGFILEON

Records and writes to a file the contents of the text window.

Command line only

How to Use It

After you turn on the log file, AutoCAD records the contents of the text window each time you enter AutoCAD, until you use LOGFILEOFF. You can use the log file for troubleshooting.

More Stuff

Each session is separated by a dashed line in the file. This file keeps on growing. So remember to sometimes get rid of the stuff you don't need. Your hard disk will thank you for it. You can change the name and location of the log file using the PREFERENCES command, Files tab.

'LTSCALE

Sets the linetype scale, which is the length of the dashes and spaces relative to the drawing unit.

Command line only

How to Use It

AutoCAD prompts you for a new scale factor and gives you the current one for reference. Type in a new number. To make the scale smaller, type in a decimal. Press Enter to end the command. AutoCAD regenerates the drawing with the new scale factor. You can also use the LINETYPE command.

More Stuff

See "Scaling, Scaling, over the Bounding Main . . ." in Chapter 4 of *AutoCAD Release 14 For Dummies*.

MASSPROP

Calculates the mass and other properties of regions or solids.

Toolbar: On the Inquiry flyout of the Standard toolbar, click the Mass Properties button.

Menu: Choose Tools⇨Inquiry⇨Mass Properties.

How to Use It

AutoCAD prompts you to select objects. They need to be regions or 3D solids. Regions are created by the REGION command, more or less for the purpose of analysis. AutoCAD struts its stuff on the text screen — and it may be a lot — and then asks whether you want to write the information to a file. If you type **y**, AutoCAD prompts you for a filename.

More Stuff

MASSPROP provides the following information for regions: Area, perimeter, bounding box, centroid (the center of the region), moments of inertia, products of inertia, radii of gyration, and principal moments of inertia. For solids, the command also provides mass and volume. Obviously, if you have no idea what this stuff is, you won't be using this command.

'MATCHPROP

Matches the properties of an object or objects to a source object.

Toolbar: Click the Match Properties button on the Standard toolbar.

Menu: Choose Modify⇨Match Properties.

MATLIB

How to Use It

Select the source object whose properties you want to copy. If you want to copy all the properties of the source object, select the destination object(s) and you're done. If you're picky, type **s** for the Settings option. Here you can choose which properties you want to copy to the destination object(s).

The properties that can be copied are layer, color, linetype, linetype scale, thickness, text style, dimension style, and hatch properties. Obviously, you can't copy a dimension style to an object that isn't a dimension, and so on — you get the idea.

More Stuff

Also called the PAINTER command.

MATLIB

Accesses a library of materials that can be imported and exported for use in rendering.

Toolbar: Click the Materials Library button on the Render toolbar.

Menu: Choose View➪Render➪Materials Library.

How to Use It

AutoCAD opens the Materials Library dialog box. The Materials List contain materials currently in your drawing. Click Purge to delete all materials that aren't attached to objects. Click Save to open the Library File dialog box and type in a name of a different materials library file, including its *.MLI* extension.

From the Library List, choose a material and then click Preview to see how the material looks on a sample sphere or cube. Click Import to add the material to the Materials List. Export moves materials from the Materials List to the Library List. Click Delete to delete materials from either list. Click Open to open the Library File dialog box, allowing you to open another materials library file.

More Stuff

See the RMAT command to attach materials to objects.

MEASURE

Puts points or blocks at specified intervals on an object (sort of like making a ruler).

Menu: Choose Draw➪Point➪Measure.

How to Use It

AutoCAD prompts you to select the object that you want to measure. Select the object, picking a point nearest the end where you want AutoCAD to start measuring. Then specify a distance, called a segment length. MEASURE puts points along the object.

Or you can select the block option, and AutoCAD puts blocks along the object.

More Stuff

Use DDPTYPE first to set the point type.

MINSERT

Inserts blocks into a rectangular array in one fell swoop.

Command line only

How to Use It

MINSERT prompts you for a block name. Type it in or press **?** to get a list. At the Insertion point prompt, specify a point. Next, type in an X scale factor (the default is 1), a Y scale factor, and a rotation angle. The rotation angle applies to the individual blocks and the entire array. Finally, AutoCAD prompts you for the number of rows and columns and the distance between them.

More Stuff

The problem with this command is that after you create the array, the members of the array cannot be changed or exploded.

See also the DDINSERT and ARRAY commands; MINSERT is essentially a combination of these two commands.

MIRROR

Makes a mirror image of an object.

 Toolbar: Click the Mirror button on the Modify toolbar.

Menu: Choose Modify➪Mirror.

MIRROR3D

How to Use It

Select the object or objects you want to mirror. AutoCAD prompts you to specify points of the mirror line. If you want the line to be at a 90-degree angle, turn on ORTHO.

AutoCAD asks whether you want to delete the old objects, that is, the objects you selected. If you type **n**, you get both the original and the mirrored version of the object. If you type **y**, AutoCAD erases the original objects, and you get just the mirrored version.

More Stuff

If the objects that you're mirroring contain text, you end up with the text reading right to left. You can tell your client to hold the drawing up to a mirror and read the text through the mirror, but you can also set the MIRRTEXT system variable to 0 to disable mirroring of text when you mirror an object. Type **mirrtext 0** on the command line and press Enter. It's a good thing to know.

MIRROR3D

Draws a mirror image in 3D space.

Menu: Choose Modify⇨3D Operation⇨Mirror 3D.

How to Use It

First, select the objects you want to mirror. Then you define the plane around which the mirror copy is created. Here are the ways you can define the plane:

3points	This is the default. Simply specify three points on the plane.
Object	Select a circle, an arc, or a 2D polyline to define the plane.
Last	Uses the last defined plane.
Zaxis	First, pick a point on the plane that you're defining. Then pick a point on the Z axis of the plane, that is, a point on a line coming out perpendicular to the plane. (This point is called a point *normal* to the plane.)
View	Pick a point on the viewing plane of the current viewport. AutoCAD uses a plane parallel to the viewing plane that goes through your point.
XY/YZ/ZX	Again, you pick a point on one of the listed planes. AutoCAD uses a plane parallel to that plane but passing through your point.

After you define your plane, AutoCAD asks you whether you want to delete the old objects, just as in the regular MIRROR command. Answer **y** or **n** and press Enter to complete the command.

MLEDIT

Edits the intersections between multiple parallel lines (multilines).

 Toolbar: Click the Edit Multiline button on the Modify II toolbar.

Menu: Choose Modify⇨Object⇨Multiline.

How to Use It

Click the image tile that displays the result you want. Some of the tiles are very similar, so you may have to try out some options before you get what you want. However, AutoCAD places a brief explanation of the image tile at the bottom of the dialog box. Click OK.

AutoCAD prompts you to select the multilines. Sometimes which multiline you select first makes a difference. AutoCAD wisely provides a **u** option to undo the results and try again.

After you're finished, AutoCAD continues to prompt you for more multilines. Press Enter to complete the command.

More Stuff

See MLINE to create multilines and MLSTYLE to manage multiline styles.

MLINE

Draws multiple parallel lines.

 Toolbar: Click the Multiline button on the Draw toolbar.

Menu: Choose Draw⇨Multiline.

How to Use It

Because multilines are so complicated, they're defined by styles. You usually create a style first and then draw your multiline. When you start MLINE, AutoCAD gives you the current justification, scale, and style and then prompts you for the first point. If you're happy with the settings, just pick a point. When AutoCAD prompts you for the next point, pick one. Continue on, picking points until you're finished and then press Enter to complete the command. The Close option connects your last multiline segment with the first. Use the Undo option after any segment to delete that segment and try again.

MLSTYLE

However, things aren't so simple. So here are the options:

Justification	Top means that the start point you pick specifies the top line. The other, parallel lines are drawn below. Zero means that the start point you pick is the center of the multiline. The other parallel lines are drawn equally distant from the start point. Bottom means that your start point specifies the bottom line. The other lines are drawn above.
Scale	This scale is a factor of the multiline style definition. That means, if you type in a scale of 3, and the style says that the lines are to be 1 unit apart, the lines will now be 3 units apart. Type in a number.
Style	Type in a multiline style or press **?** to get a listing.

After you complete the options, you can start drawing multilines.

More Stuff

See MLEDIT to edit multilines and MLSTYLE to manage multiline styles.

For the Scale option, you can type negative values to flip the order of the lines. Typing **0** turns the multiline into a single line.

For more on multilines, see "Multilines (lines aplenty)" in Chapter 6 of *AutoCAD Release 14 For Dummies*.

MLSTYLE

Manages styles for multilines.

Menu: Choose Format⇨Multiline Style.

How to Use It

This command opens the Multiline Styles dialog box. The top section, called Multiline Style, manages the styles. If the style you want already exists, select it from the Current drop-down list box to make it current. Then click OK and go and make multilines.

Create a new style by following these steps:

1. Type a name in the Name text box. It can be up to 31 characters with no spaces.

2. Click Add to add the style.

3. Click the Element Properties button to open the Element Properties dialog box. Elements are the lines, and they're defined by their offset (distance) from the multiline start point, their color, and their linetype.

MLSTYLE

4. If you don't want the existing lines, select them and click Delete.

5. In the Offset text box, type in an offset amount. If you want a line right at the start point, your first offset is 0.

6. Click Add. The offset appears in the Elements box near the top of the Element Properties dialog box.

7. Click the new element and choose Color. AutoCAD opens the Select Color dialog box, which also appears when you use the DDCOLOR command. (I'm sure that you're reading this book from cover to cover and have already read about DDCOLOR.) Select the color you want or the BYLAYER or BYBLOCK options and click OK to return to the Element Properties dialog box.

8. Make sure the element you want to change is highlighted in the Elements box and choose Linetype. AutoCAD opens the Select Linetype dialog box. You can find instructions for it under the LINETYPE command. Select the linetype you want or the BYLAYER or BYBLOCK options and click OK. You're back to the Element Properties dialog box again.

9. Repeat Steps 5 through 8 for other lines. Click OK when you're done with the Element Properties dialog box.

10. Back at the Multiline Styles dialog box, click Multiline Properties to open the Multiline Properties dialog box.

11. Click the Display joints check box if you want to show a short cross-line at the vertices of the multiline segments. This display gives an effect somewhat like stained glass.

12. The Caps section controls how the start and end of the multiline are finished off, that is, how you put a cap on the multiline. Choose from Line, which is straight across; Outer arc, which makes a nice semicircle connecting the outer lines; Inner arcs, which makes nice semicircles connecting the inner elements; and Angle, where you can specify lines at an angle.

13. Go to the Fill section. Choose On to turn background fill on.

14. Click Color to select a color for the background fill. You get the Select Color dialog box again.

15. Click OK to return to the Multiline Styles dialog box.

16. Under Description, type in a suitable description. This description can be pretty long (255 characters) and can include spaces.

17. Click Save. Click Save again in the Save Multiline Style dialog box to save the style in `acad.mln`.

18. Click Load, choose the style from the list and then click OK. Remember this step or else you won't be able to use your new multiline style later. This process works a bit differently from other loaded, named objects, such as linetypes.

19. Click OK again to complete the command. You're finally done!

Whew! That's a lot of steps. Are you sure you still want to draw multilines? But after you've created the style, drawing the multilines is fairly simple (see the MLINE command).

More Stuff

When creating elements, use positive offset numbers to create lines above the middle of the multiline and negative offset numbers to create lines below.

In the Multiline Styles dialog box, use Rename to rename a multiline style.

For more on multilines, see "Multilines (lines aplenty)" in Chapter 6 of *AutoCAD Release 14 For Dummies*.

MOVE

Moves objects.

Toolbar: Click the Move button on the Modify toolbar.

Menu: Choose Modify⇨Move.

How to Use It

First, select your object or objects. AutoCAD prompts for a Base point or displacement. Pick a base point. AutoCAD then prompts you for a second point of displacement that shows the distance and location from the base point. You can pick a point, use an object snap, or type in a coordinate, such as @–2,0. AutoCAD moves your objects as indicated by the distance and direction between the two points.

To use the displacement method, just type the displacement at the first prompt. If you're typing X,Y coordinates, do *not* use @, as in –2,0. At the second prompt, press Enter.

More Stuff

You can use grips to move objects, too. See DDGRIPS.

MSPACE

Switches from paper space to model space.

Menu: Choose View➪Model Space (Floating).

On the status bar, double-click PAPER to toggle it to MODEL.

How to Use It

Because you ordinarily draw in model space, the only reason you'd switch to model space is if you've previously switched to paper space. You switched to paper space to create floating viewports containing different views of your model using the MVIEW command. (I know, floating viewports reminds you of being weightless in a spaceship and floating by a viewport, looking at some asteroid. But sooner or later, you're probably going to come down to Earth and deal with this stuff.) You have two ways to work in model space:

- ✦ If the TILEMODE system variable is off (0), you still see your paper space layout but can work on your model in one of the floating viewports.

- ✦ If the TILEMODE system variable is on (1), you return to regular model space with no sign of the paper space layout.

More Stuff

See Chapter 13 in *AutoCAD Release 14 For Dummies* for more on using paper space.

MTEXT

Creates text in paragraph form.

Toolbar: Click the Multiline Text button on the Draw toolbar.

Menu: Choose Draw➪Text➪Multiline Text.

How to Use It

At the first prompt, specify an insertion point for the text. Then AutoCAD prompts you for the other corner. Picking this second point creates a text boundary within which the text flows. (A bunch of options exist that you can ignore, since you can set them more easily in the Multiline Text Editor.) AutoCAD opens the Multiline Text Editor. Type your text and click OK.

MVIEW

The Multiline Text Editor has three tabs:

Character	Specify the font, height, and color. You can also choose from bold, italic, and underline styles. Not all fonts support bold and italic. To stack fractions (where one character is on top of another), type in the fraction, highlight it, and click the Stack button. To add special symbols, click Symbol and choose from the list. Choose Other from the Symbol list to open Windows Character Map, which contains several fonts of symbols.
Properties	Specify properties of the paragraph as a whole, such as text style, justification, paragraph width, and rotation.
Find/Replace	Use this tab to find specified text. If you want, you can replace the text with new text.

Click Import Text to open the Import Text File dialog box. Locate any .txt or .rtf (Rich Text Format) file and click Open. The text appears in the text box.

More Stuff

Multiline text, also called paragraph text, is one object. In single line text (created using TEXT or DTEXT), each line is a separate object.

MVIEW

Manages floating viewports. Floating viewports are created in paper space. The viewports themselves are actual objects that you can move, resize, and delete. Their purpose is to set up a final set of views of your objects for printing. They're usually used for 3D objects but can be used for 2D objects as well.

Menu: Choose View➪Floating Viewports.

How to Use It

Before you can use this command, you need to turn off the TILEMODE system variable. The easiest way is to double-click TILE on the status bar. This action also automatically puts you into paper space and makes your drawing disappear! To bring it back, use MVIEW. Choose the number of viewports that you want from the submenu. If you choose 2 or 3, AutoCAD gives you further options to specify how the viewports are configured. The Fit option is used if you want the viewports to fill the entire display. Otherwise, pick two points to specify the outside corners of all the viewports. The ON and OFF options turn viewports on and off.

More Stuff

If you have saved a viewport configuration using VPORTS, you can restore them using MVIEW. In other words, you can use the same configuration for tiled and floating viewports.

MVSETUP

Sets up a drawing including specifications for floating viewports. Only for the brave-at-heart!

Command line only

How to Use It

If TILEMODE is on (the default), you use MVSETUP to set up a drawing. AutoCAD asks you if you want to enable paper space just in case. If you want to set up a drawing, just say no. MVSETUP walks you through the following prompts:

Units type	Choose a type of units of measurement (equivalent to using DDUNITS).
Scale factor	AutoCAD lists common scale factors. Type a scale factor.
Paper width	Type a width. This setting is equivalent to the X coordinate you would use with the LIMITS command.
Paper height	Type a height. This setting is equivalent to the Y coordinate you would use with the LIMITS command.

On the other hand, if TILEMODE is off, here are your options:

Align	Pans the view in a viewport to align it with a base point of the active viewport. The suboptions are Angled, Horizontal, Vertical alignment, and Rotate view.
Create	Start with this option to create and delete viewports. If you press Enter, you get to create them. The suboptions are Single, Standard Engineering, and Array of viewports. Select the Delete suboption to delete a viewport. Try the Standard Engineering option to get a trial run of what the command does.
Scale	Adjusts the scale factor of the objects in the viewports. The scale factor is the ratio between the paper space size and the scale of the objects. The suboptions enable you to set the scale uniformly, for all viewports, or interactively, which means one at a time.

Options	The suboptions enable you to set a layer for the title block, reset limits after a title block has been inserted, specify paper space units, such as inches or millimeters, and choose whether the title block should be an xref or inserted into the drawing.
Title block	This option inserts a title block and sets the drawing origin. When you set the title block, you can choose from a menu of standard sizes. You can choose one and get a default border or choose Add and enter a title block description, filename, and usable area (lower-left and upper-right corners). Selecting the Origin suboption enables you to relocate the origin point for the drawing.

AutoCAD, in its great wisdom, knows that this is difficult stuff and offers you Undo options at each level.

More Stuff

See the MSPACE and PSPACE commands for details about paper space. See Chapter 13 in *AutoCAD Release 14 For Dummies* for more on MVSETUP.

NEW

Creates a new drawing.

 Toolbar: On the Standard toolbar, click the New button.

Menu: Choose File⇨New.

How to Use It

AutoCAD opens the Create New Drawing dialog box. Here you can choose to use a wizard to set up the new drawing, open a drawing based on a template, or start from scratch using default settings.

OFFSET

Creates new objects at a specified distance from an existing object.

 Toolbar: On the Modify toolbar, click the Offset button.

Menu: Choose Modify⇨Offset.

How to Use It

First, type the distance of the new object from the existing one. Then AutoCAD prompts you to select an object. When you do so, AutoCAD asks which side. Pick a point on the side of the object where you want the new copy to appear.

You have an option to pick a point through which the new object passes. This option is a simple way to indicate both the offset distance and the side where the new object appears. Type **t** for the through option, select the object to offset, and pick the Through point.

Either way, AutoCAD continues to prompt you for more offset opportunities. Press Enter to end the command.

OOPS

This cute little command, the only one with a sense of humor, restores erased objects. OOPS erases only the last erased object but does so even after you've used intervening commands.

Command line only

How to Use It

After you erase something, just use OOPS to get it back.

More Stuff

U and UNDO can also be used to reverse the effect of an ERASE command, if used immediately.

OPEN

Opens an existing drawing.

Toolbar: On the Standard toolbar, click the Open button.

Menu: Choose File➪Open.

How to Use It

OPEN displays the Select File dialog box which includes a nice Preview box that shows you what a drawing looks like when you highlight it. Navigate to the drawing's location using the Look in drop-down box. Double-click the drawing's folder in the large box if necessary. When you find the drawing, double-click it or click it once and click Open.

110 OPENURL

Click Find File to open the Browse/Search dialog box. The browse tab displays small drawing images. The search tab enables you to specify a file type, date, or search pattern.

If you know the name of the drawing but aren't sure where it is on the labyrinth that is your hard disk, type the drawing name in the File name box and click Locate. AutoCAD only looks in the search path, however, which you can set using the PREFERENCES command.

OPENURL

See INTERNET UTILITIES.

'ORTHO

Restricts the cursor to horizontal and vertical directions. Very helpful in creating nice straight lines.

On the status bar, double-click Ortho.

How to Use It

You just double-click to turn it on or off. You can also use the DDRMODES command.

More Stuff

If you're using a User Coordinate System or snap rotation, ORTHO is set horizontal and vertical to those settings.

'OSNAP

Sets object snap modes that continue in effect until you turn them off. These are called Running Object Snap modes.

Toolbar: On the Object Snap flyout of the Standard toolbar, click the Object Snap Settings button.

Menu: Choose Tools⇨Object Snap Settings.

How to Use It

AutoCAD opens the Osnap Settings dialog box. In the Select Settings section, click the object snaps you want. Or click Clear All to turn off all the object snaps. You can set the size of the target box (*aperture*) that you use to select objects using the slider bar.

Use the AutoSnap tab to manage Release 14's new AutoSnap feature — you can turn off the Snap Tips, change the marker color, and so on. Part I explains this new feature further.

More Stuff

See the "Turning on running object snaps" section in Chapter 3 of *AutoCAD Release 14 For Dummies*. Note that if you turn on the OSNAP button on the status bar and no running object snaps are set, AutoCAD opens the Osnap Settings dialog box for you, as if to say, "And which osnaps would you like today?"

PAINTER

See MATCHPROP.

'PAN

Moves the drawing display so that you get to see something new and different.

Toolbar: On the Standard toolbar, click the Pan button.

Menu: Choose View➪Pan.

How to Use It

Real-time pan is the new default. Just press the mouse button and drag in the direction you want to pan. You must press Esc or Enter, or start a command, to exit this mode. Right-clicking opens up the same menu as for real-time zoom where you can change to real-time zoom or choose Exit to exit real-time zoom and pan mode.

More Stuff

You can also use the scroll bars to pan vertically and horizontally. To use the type of pan you remember from prior releases, choose View➪Pan➪Point from the menu. Then pick the first point and a second point. AutoCAD moves the drawing display according to the distance and angle between the two points.

PEDIT

Edits polylines and 3D polygon meshes.

Toolbar: On the Modify II toolbar, click the Edit Polyline button.

Menu: Choose Modify➪Object➪Polyline.

PEDIT

How to Use It

Select a 2D polyline. AutoCAD offers the following options:

Close/Open		If the polyline is closed, you can choose Open to remove the closing segment. If it's open, choose Close to close it.
Join		If other objects are connected to the polyline, you can join them into the Polyline Club with this option. Choose Join and select the attached objects. The objects never decline to join, unlike some people.
Width		Specify a width for the entire polyline.
Edit vertex		Offers you the following list of submenu options. PEDIT puts an X at the first vertex so that you know which vertex you're editing.
	Next	Moves the X to the next vertex. It stops at the last vertex.
	Previous	Moves the X marker to the previous vertex. If you've used Next to get to the last vertex, this is how you get back to the beginning.
	Break	Breaks the polyline into two pieces. However, this offers you a sub-submenu. (Are you following me here?) If you just type **go**, AutoCAD breaks the polyline. However, AutoCAD holds the current vertex, and if you use Next or Previous to specify the other end of the break and then use **go**, AutoCAD breaks the polyline between the two vertices, leaving a hole.
	Insert	Adds a new vertex after the vertex marked with the X. You pick a point for the location of the new vertex.
	Move	Moves the vertex with the X. (Did you notice the rhyme?) You specify the new location.
	Regen	Regenerates the polyline.
	Straighten	This option offers the same sub-submenu as Break and works the same way. Replaces the vertices with a straight line.
	Tangent	Marks a tangent direction to the vertex with the X, which can be used for curve fitting, that is, the Fit and Spline options. You specify a point or angle to indicate the direction of the tangent.
	Width	Edits the start and end widths for the segment after the marked vertex. Type in a starting and ending width. Use the Regen option to see the results.
	eXit	Exits the Edit vertex submenu and returns you to the original PEDIT prompt.

Fit	Turns the polyline into a smooth curve.
Spline	A spline is a mathematically constructed curve that uses the vertices of your polyline as the frame of the curve. You can control which type of spline you create using system variables. At any rate, just choose this option, and AutoCAD makes your spline.
Decurve	Undoes the results of the Fit and Spline options.
Ltype gen	Select ON to generate a linetype continuously through the vertices of the polyline. Select OFF to start each vertex with a dash. This option is meaningless if you're using a continuous linetype.
Undo	Undoes operations one-by-one back to the beginning of your PEDIT session (which may seem like ages ago).
eXit	Exits PEDIT.

More Stuff

If you select a 3D polyline curve (created with the 3DPOLY command), the prompts are slightly different, but not much. If you select a 3D polygon mesh, you also get similar prompts, but with more Edit vertex options because you can move the vertex in three dimensions, using the M and N dimensions.

How do you turn ordinary lines and arcs into a polyline? Use this command and select attached lines and arcs. AutoCAD informs you that this is not a polyline and asks whether you want to turn it into one. Type **y** and there you go!

PLAN

Shows the plan view of a User Coordinate System (UCS).

Menu: Choose View⇨3D Viewpoint⇨Plan View.

How to Use It

The plan view is the one looking down from the top, the regular, old 2D way of looking at things. Use the Current option or press Enter to get the plan view of the current UCS.

Use the Named option (called Ucs on the command line) to restore a named UCS that you've saved. Type in the name. If you forget it, type **?**, and AutoCAD lists name options for you.

The World option returns you to the World Coordinate System.

PLINE

Draws a 2D polyline, which is a connected series of lines and arcs that is one object.

Toolbar: On the Draw toolbar, click the Polyline button.

Menu: Choose Draw⇨Polyline.

How to Use It

AutoCAD prompts you for your start point. Specify a point. The next prompt offers the following options:

Endpoint of line		This option is the default, and when you pick a point, you get a line.
Arc		Type **a** to switch into Arc mode. This option has its own submenu.
	Endpoint of arc	This option is the default. Pick a point.
	Angle	Type in an included angle for the arc. A positive angle draws the arc counterclockwise. A negative angle goes clockwise. Then you get the rest of the standard options for drawing an arc (see the ARC command).
	Center	Specify a point for the center of the arc. Again, you then get the rest of the standard arc options.
	CLose	Closes your polyline with an arc.
	Direction	Pick a point to indicate a direction from the start point of the arc. Then pick an endpoint.
	Halfwidth	The halfwidth is the distance from the center of the polyline to its edge. Usually, you type in a distance. You can pick different starting and ending halfwidths for a tapered arc segment. I'm not sure how useful this is for drafting, but the results look pretty.
	Line	Returns PEDIT to line mode.
	Radius	Pick a point for the radius of the arc. AutoCAD continues to give you standard arc prompts so that you can finish the arc. (Don't delay finishing the arc, because it's going to start raining any day now.)
	Second pt	Complete the arc by specifying second points and endpoints.
	Undo	Undoes the last arc segment you created. You *never* need this option!
	Width	Like halfwidth, but you specify the whole width instead of the halfwidth.

Close	Draws a line from the end to the start of the polyline, closing it.
Halfwidth	See the Arc submenu options.
Length	Picking a point specifies the length of the next line segment, which is drawn in the same direction as the previous one.
Undo	See the Arc submenu options.
Width	See the Arc submenu options.

More Stuff

The PEDIT command edits polylines. For much more on polylines, see "Polylines (wanna crackerline?)" in Chapter 6 of *AutoCAD Release 14 For Dummies*.

PLOT

Plots or prints a drawing.

Toolbar: On the Standard toolbar, click the Print button.

Menu: Choose File➪Print.

How to Use It

AutoCAD opens the Print/Plot Configuration dialog box. It's a big one, with several sublevels of dialog boxes, too, but here goes.

Try a full preview (explained later in this section) first. If everything looks hunky-dory, click OK to plot. (You're very lucky!)

The Device and Default Information section shows you the current plotter or printer. Click the Device and Default Selection button to open the dialog box of the same name. That dialog box enables you to select your plotter or printer, save all these complex plot configurations to a file so that you don't have to do it each time, and make some plotter/printer changes depending on the plotter or printer you have.

The Pen Parameters section enables you to set the parameters for plotters with multiple pens and other pen options. Click the Pen Assignments button to open a dialog box. Pen assignments are for plotters with more than one pen. The concept to understand here is that you base the assignment on an object's color. For each color you assign a pen, linetype, speed, and pen width (except that these days you hardly ever use the linetype, speed, or pen width options). Click Optimization to set options that optimize pen motion in order to reduce plot time.

PLOT

The Additional Parameters section enables you to specify what part of the drawing you want to print.

Display	Plots what is on-screen.
Extents	Plots the entire drawing. It's like ZOOM with the Extents option.
Limits	Plots the drawing as defined by the LIMITS command.
View	Plots a view you've saved using the DDVIEW or VIEW command.
Window	Plots any window you select. Click the Window button to return to the drawing to specify the two corners of the window you want to plot.

On the right side of the Additional Parameters section, Text Fill is on by default, but you can uncheck it to save ink and time. Choose Hide Lines to hide lines in 3D objects that would normally be hidden from view. Choose Adjust Area Fill if you have solid-filled objects and need a very high level of accuracy. AutoCAD adjusts the pen width so that the fill doesn't go outside the boundaries. (Remember learning to color within the lines in kindergarten?) Click Plot to File to plot to a file instead of to a plotter. When you choose the Plot to File check box, the File Name button darkens, and you can choose a filename other than the default, which is the name of your drawing with a .plt extension. If you have set up plot spooling, you can choose Autospool to queue up the plot on your plotter or printer.

In the Paper Size and Orientation section, you specify whether your drawing units represent inches or millimeters. The orientation icon shows whether you're in landscape or portrait mode. The Size button opens up the Paper Size dialog box, where you can choose from standard sizes of paper or type in your own size.

The next section is called Scale, Rotation, and Origin. The scale is the units plotted for each unit on the drawing. Type in the number of plotted units in the left box and the number of drawing units in the right box. For example, if you want to plot a drawing of a table that is 24 x 36-inches, and you want it to fit on an 8 $^1/_2$ x 11-inch piece of paper, using a 1=4 scale results in a table that is 6 x 9-inches on paper. You can use inches and feet, such as, 1"=1'.

Click Scale to Fit to scale the drawing to fit the paper size that you've selected.

If you're having trouble figuring out the scale, click the Scale to Fit check box and see what AutoCAD calculates. This calculation gives you a ballpark figure to work with, and you can change the scale to something similar that fits standard scales.

POLYGON

Click the Rotation and Origin button to open the Plot Rotation and Origin dialog box. Here you pick the plot rotation and plot origin, which is usually, but not always, 0,0.

Finally, the last section is Plot Preview. Choose Partial to see just a rectangle representing your precious drawing in a (hopefully) bigger rectangle representing the paper. Choose Full to get an accurate image of your drawing, including a Pan and Zoom button that works like 'ZOOM with the Dynamic option. Click End Preview.

Click OK. Load paper in the plotter. At the prompt, press Enter, and the plot starts.

More Stuff

See Chapter 12 of *AutoCAD Release 14 For Dummies*, for a full chapter's worth on plotting.

POINT

Draws a point.

 Toolbar: On the Draw toolbar, click the Point button.

Menu: Choose Draw➪Point➪Single Point, or Draw➪Point➪Multiple Point.

How to Use It

AutoCAD prompts you to specify a point (meaning a coordinate) and then draws a point (meaning a point object).

More Stuff

Unless you chose Single Point from the menu, you have to press Esc to end the command. Use DDPTYPE to determine how points appear.

POLYGON

Draws a polygon using polylines.

 Toolbar: On the Draw toolbar, click the Polygon button.

Menu: Choose Draw➪Polygon.

How to Use It

POLYGON asks you for the number of sides. You can type any number from 3 to 1,024. Next, you specify the center. Now comes the interesting part. Your choices are:

Inscribed in circle	You specify a circle radius. The vertices of the polygon will be on the circle (so that the polygon will be inside the circle).
Circumscribed about circle	You specify a circle radius. The midpoints of each side of the polygon will lie on the circle (so that the polygon will be outside the circle).

The circle doesn't really exist; it's just a way of defining the polygon.

Instead of specifying the center at the first prompt, you can type **e**, for edge, and then pick two points that define the endpoints of the first edge.

More Stuff

Because the polygon is a polyline, you can use PEDIT to edit it.

PREFERENCES

Sets your preferences for various aspects of AutoCAD.

Menu: Choose Tools⇨Preferences.

How to Use It

This command displays the Preferences dialog box, which contains the following tabs:

Files	Here you specify the all-important search path so that AutoCAD can find hatch and linetype files, and so on. The Project Files Search Path is where AutoCAD searches for xrefs. The other types of files are fairly self-explanatory. Use the Browse command to navigate to the paths and files you need.
Performance	Sets how 3D models are displayed, sets DRAGMODE, and a few other performance-related items.
Compatibility	You can turn off the Start Up dialog box here, return to the AutoCAD classic (sounds like a soft drink) keyboard shortcuts — such as Ctrl+C for cancel instead of Copy to Clipboard. Some other technical settings are here, too.

General	Here you set how often AutoCAD automatically saves your drawing — very important! You can also turn the log file on or off, turn off the creation of backup (*.bak) files whenever you save a drawing, turn off the preview image you see when you open a file, and so on.
Display	You can turn on the old screen menu, turn off the scroll bars if you never use them (most people don't), change the size of the command line area, and change the colors and fonts of the screen.
Pointer	Here you configure your pointing device (mouse or digitizer) and change the size of the crosshairs cursor.
Printer	Here you configure your printer/plotter.
Profiles	Use this tab to manage profiles which are collections of settings that you define using the PREFERENCES command. This way, you can quickly change a whole bunch of settings to work in a different way. (Or maybe two of you use the same computer and like to work differently.) You can change the current profile or create a new one by clicking copy and then making changes using the other tabs of the Preferences dialog box. Then click Export to save the profile as an .arg file. After you have your profiles, choose one and click Set Current to use it.

PSPACE

Switches to paper space. This concept enables you to create floating viewports to show various views of your drawing as well as to set up a title block and border and, in general, prepare a layout for plotting.

Menu: Choose View➪Paper Space.

Double-click MODEL on the status bar.

Switching to paper space by using the menu or the status bar automatically turns off TILEMODE (tiled viewports).

How to Use It

If you use the status bar or menu, AutoCAD automatically turns off TILEMODE for you. Use PSPACE to work on the layout, for example, create or move floating viewports or change their layer.

More Stuff

If you type this command at the command line, you have to set the TILEMODE system variable to 0 (off). Double-click TILE on the status bar.

See also MSPACE and MVIEW.

PURGE

Removes unused blocks, layers, dimension styles, text styles, multiline styles, shapes, and linetypes from the drawing database, reducing the size of the drawing.

Menu: Choose File➪Drawing Utilities➪Purge.

How to Use It

You can choose a specific option to purge or choose the All option to get rid of everything. AutoCAD lists the names of unused layers, blocks, and so on. AutoCAD then asks, Verify each name to be purged? No/<Yes>:. Type **n** and press Enter to purge everything without having to review each item (a new feature for Release 14). Otherwise, for each item that you want to purge, type **y** @e.

More Stuff

You may have to use PURGE more than once to get to nested blocks and so on.

QSAVE

Saves your drawing.

Toolbar: On the Standard toolbar, click the Save button.

Menu: Choose File➪Save.

How to Use It

AutoCAD saves your drawing to your hard disk. If you haven't named your drawing, QSAVE opens the Save Drawing As dialog box so that you can type a name.

More Stuff

Use this command a lot. *Not* using this command is *not* safe!

'QTEXT

Turns text objects into rectangles to reduce display and plotting time.

Command line only

How to Use It

Type **on** or **off.** When you turn on QTEXT (it stands for quick text), text is displayed as just a rectangle around the text location. Then type **regen** and press Enter to see the result.

More Stuff

If you leave QTEXT on when you plot, all you get is rectangles, so don't forget to turn it off before you plot! (QTEXT may be useful for a draft plot, however.)

QUIT

Exits AutoCAD.

Menu: Choose File➪Exit.

Click the Close box at the top right of the title bar.

How to Use It

If you haven't made any changes to your drawing, AutoCAD throws you out unceremoniously. If you have made changes, AutoCAD reminds you to save your changes, if you want, before quitting.

RAY

Creates a line with a starting point that extends to infinity.

Menu: Choose Draw➪Ray.

How to Use It

At the `From point:` prompt, pick a start point of the ray. AutoCAD prompts you for a Through point. Specify another point. The ray continues on, and on, and on.... AutoCAD continues to ask you for Through points so that you can make other rays starting from the same point. Press Enter to end the command.

122 RECOVER

More Stuff

Luckily, commands such as ZOOM Extents ignore rays; otherwise, you'd get some unusual results. Also, the PLOT command doesn't expect an infinite-size sheet of paper — it's all a mirage.

See the section "Rays and infinite lines (Buck Rogers, watch out!)" in Chapter 6 of *AutoCAD Release 14 For Dummies*.

RECOVER

Tries to repair a damaged drawing.

Menu: Choose File➪Drawing Utilities➪Recover.

How to Use It

Use this command only after you receive some sort of error message, such as the famous AutoCAD FATAL ERROR message. (It's okay; I've gotten lots of error messages, and I'm still alive to write this book.) In other words, you can't open the drawing.

Start a new drawing, and use the RECOVER command. AutoCAD opens the Recover Drawing File dialog box. Select the file from the list. AutoCAD starts recovering the drawing, displaying a report on-screen as it works.

More Stuff

See also the AUDIT command, which repairs drawings that you can open. Not every drawing can be recovered. If your drawings are important, get in the habit of making backup copies to floppy diskettes.

When you can't get into a drawing, you should first go and rename the drawing's *.bak file and any temporary files (auto.sv$) so that they have *.dwg extensions but different file names. You may be able to open one of them. Another trick is to open a spanking new drawing and try to insert the drawing (using DDINSERT).

RECTANG

Draws a rectangle using a polyline.

Toolbar: On the Draw toolbar, click the Rectangle button.

Menu: Choose Draw➪Rectangle.

How to Use It

This command is easy. AutoCAD prompts you for the two corners of the rectangle. Specify two points and — poof! — you have a rectangle.

More Stuff

Release 14 now includes options that enable you to chamfer or fillet the rectangle, as well as give it thickness (3D), elevation (3D), or thickness.

REDO

Redoes whatever the preceding U or UNDO command undid.

Toolbar: On the Standard toolbar, click the Redo button.

Menu: Choose Edit⇨Redo.

How to Use It

When you use the command, AutoCAD redoes whatever you undid with the U or UNDO command.

More Stuff

You need to use this command *immediately* after using the U or UNDO command. Go straight to this command; do not pass Go; do not collect $200. See section "The Way You Undo the Things You Do" in Chapter 5 of *AutoCAD Release 14 For Dummies*.

'REDRAWALL

Redisplays the drawing (including all viewports you may have), removing blip marks and wayward pixels left behind by your editing.

Toolbar: On the Standard toolbar, click the Redraw All button.

Menu: Choose View⇨Redraw.

How to Use It

Just use the command; AutoCAD obeys.

More Stuff

Also, the REDRAW command (on the command line only) redraws only the current viewport.

REGEN

Regenerates the drawing, re-computes coordinates, and re-indexes the database.

Menu: Choose View➪Regen.

How to Use It

Type the command; AutoCAD obeys.

More Stuff

REGEN takes longer than REDRAW; it updates many changes that may have taken place since the last time you did a REGEN. Use REGENALL (View➪Regen All) to regenerate all viewports.

REGENAUTO

Manages the way that AutoCAD regenerates drawings.

Command line only

How to Use It

Type **on** or **off**. On means that AutoCAD regenerates automatically when needed — but much less often than for previous releases of AutoCAD. Sometimes, regeneration is time-consuming (you can use it as an opportunity for a coffee break), so that you can set the command to off. Thereafter, each time AutoCAD needs to regen, it asks you whether it should proceed. You can type **y** or **n**, but if you say no, AutoCAD wimps out on you and cancels the command.

REGION

Creates a region object, which is a 2D closed area.

 **Toolbar:** On the Draw toolbar, click the Region button.

Menu: Choose Draw➪Region.

How to Use It

AutoCAD prompts you to select objects. You can select closed polylines, lines, circles, ellipses, and splines. AutoCAD ignores internal objects as best it can and converts your objects to a region, deleting the original objects in the process. You can't use self-intersecting shapes (such as figure 8s).

More Stuff

AutoCAD can do certain things with regions that it can't with the original objects. For example, you can use the MASSPROP command to analyze certain properties, and you can hatch them. Finally, you can use INTERSECT, SUBTRACT, and UNION to play around with sets of regions (called *composite regions*).

See also the BOUNDARY command, which can also create regions. See the BHATCH command if you want to hatch a region.

REINIT

Reinitializes the digitizer input/output port (such as COM1); your digitizer; and acad.pgp, which holds command shortcut definitions.

Command line only

How to Use It

In the dialog box, check the item you want to reinitialize and click OK.

More Stuff

Use this command only if you changed your hardware configuration or the acad.pgp file during a drawing session.

RENAME

See also the DDRENAME command, which does the same thing in a dialog box.

RENDER

Shades 3D solid or surface objects, using lights, scenes, and materials. Gives a semi-realistic appearance to your objects.

RENDER

 Toolbar: On the Render toolbar, click the Render button.

Menu: Choose View⇨Render⇨Render.

How to Use It

 Before you render, you usually create lights with the LIGHT command and a scene with the SCENE command. You can render without any preparation, however; RENDER uses the current view and a default light source.

 This command opens the Render dialog box. The Rendering Type drop-down list now includes AutoCAD Render, Photo Raytrace, and Photo Real. Choose the type of renderer you want.

- ✦ *Render* is AutoCAD's original renderer. It's simplest and fastest.

- ✦ *Photo Real* creates images line by line. It can display bitmap images, create transparent materials, and make shadows based on volume.

- ✦ *Photo Raytrace* traces rays of light. It's best for generating precise reflections, refraction, and shadows.

The Scene to Render box lists any scenes that you defined. The current view is listed as an option. Choose the one you want.

In the Rendering Procedure section, check one of the options if you wish. Query for Selections means that AutoCAD asks you to select objects. Use this to test a rendering on one or more objects — this saves rendering time. Choose Crop Window to choose a window to render. Choose Skip Render Dialog to render immediately without even opening the dialog box (the next time).

Set the Light Icon Scale to set the size of the icons represent lights you've inserted into your scene. Use the drawing scale factor so you can see the light icons clearly in your drawing.

Set the Smoothing Angle. The smoothing angle determines the angle at which AutoCAD assumes an edge as opposed to a smooth curve. Angles greater than the smoothing angle are considered to be edges and are not smoothed. The default is 45 degrees. A lower angle results in more edges.

The Rendering Options section enables you to select Smooth Shading. This option blends the colors across adjacent surfaces. Choose Apply Materials to use materials that you imported from the materials library and attached to objects (see the MATLIB and RMAT commands). Check Shadows to create shadows. You can only create shadows with the Photo Real and Photo Raytrace renderers. Remember that shadows take much longer to render.

Check Render Cache to save rendering information in a file. AutoCAD can reuse this information for subsequent renderings, saving time.

Click More Options (as if you wanted even more) to get to the AutoCAD Render Options dialog box. The options depend on the type of renderer that you've chosen. For example, if you've chosen the plain-vanilla Render, you can choose between two types of rendering: Phong, which results in higher-quality renderings and better highlights; or Gouraud, which results in faster but lower-quality renderings.

For all renderers, you have two Face Controls options. The rendering process analyzes which faces are facing front and which are facing back. When you draw a 3D face counterclockwise, RENDER counts it as a front face and renders it. Back faces need not be rendered because they aren't seen in the final rendering. When you choose the Discard Back Faces option, RENDER doesn't calculate them, thereby speeding the rendering process. Choosing the Back Face Normal is Negative option reverses the faces AutoCAD considers to be back faces. This option is for those of you who draw everything clockwise. Click OK to return to the Render dialog box.

The Destination section selects the location of the rendered image. If you want to see the results, the location must be either Viewport (the default) or Render Window. The Render Window has its own special menu and toolbar, which enables you to open an image file and save the rendered image to it. You also can copy the image to the Windows Clipboard. And you can render to a file.

Use the Sub Sampling drop-down box to set the sampling of pixels that AutoCAD renders. The default, 1:1, renders all the pixels. Try a lower ratio for faster or preliminary renderings.

Click Render to render the selected scene.

Redraw the screen to return to your original models.

More Stuff

The other commands related to rendering are LIGHT, MATLIB, RMAT, RPREF, SAVEIMG, SCENE, and STATS. Release 14 now includes all of AutoVision which used to be a separate program.

REVOLVE

Draws a solid by revolving a 2D object around an axis.

 Toolbar: On the Solids toolbar, click the Revolve button.

Menu: Choose Draw➪Solids➪Revolve.

REVSURF

How to Use It

First, you need an object to revolve. The object can be any closed polyline, polygon, circle, ellipse, closed spline, donut, or region. The object cannot have crossing or intersecting parts. Next, you need to decide what your axis is. You may want to draw a line so that you can select it to specify the axis.

AutoCAD asks you to select objects. You can revolve only one object at a time, so select one object.

Next, you need to specify the axis, using the following options:

Start point of axis	This option is the default. Specify a point; AutoCAD asks for the endpoint of the axis.
Object	Select an existing line for your axis.
X	This option revolves the object around the positive X axis.
Y	This option revolves the object around the positive Y axis.

For all options, AutoCAD then asks whether you want to revolve a full circle (360 degrees) or a specified angle. Your answer completes the command.

More Stuff

If several lines and arcs make up the shape that you want to revolve, you can use REGION to convert them to one object. Alternatively, see the tip under the PEDIT command for details on turning separate lines and arcs into a polyline.

REVSURF

Draws a surface by revolving a line, arc, circle, or polyline around an axis.

Toolbar: On the Surface toolbar, click the Revolved Surface button.

Menu: Choose Draw⇨Surfaces⇨Revolved Surface.

How to Use It

First, you need a *path curve,* which means a line, arc, circle, or polyline. The path curve doesn't really have to curve; it can be made up of straight-line segments. Next, you need an object to be your axis (a line or polyline). Create those first (that's the hard part) and then use the command. AutoCAD prompts you to select a path curve and then the axis of revolution.

Now you need to supply the start angle (the default is 0) and the included angle (the default is a full circle).

RMAT

Defines materials and attaches them to objects for the purpose of rendering them.

Toolbar: On the Render toolbar, click the Materials button.

Menu: Choose View➪Render➪Materials.

How to Use It

Before using this command, use the MATLIB command to load materials from a materials library.

RMAT opens the Materials dialog box. On the left is a list of available materials, which always includes the *GLOBAL* default material. In the middle is a preview box for looking at your beautiful materials.

Defining a material

To create a new material from scratch, choose a type of material from the drop-down box beneath the New button. Choose granite, marble, or wood if you want your new material to look like granite, marble, or wood. Otherwise, choose Standard. Click New. The New Standard (or Granite or Marble or Wood) Material dialog box opens. Type a name for your material. On the left of the dialog box are the attributes you need to define. (They vary according to the type of material you chose — the main attributes are listed below.) Select these options one at a time and, for each option, complete the Value and Color settings in the center of the dialog box.

Color/Pattern	This option sets the diffuse color — the base color that the object reflects. Value sets the intensity of the color. To set color, you must deselect the By ACI button. If you choose a bitmap at the bottom of the dialog box, you define a pattern instead of a color.
Ambient	This option sets the color reflected from ambient light. (See the LIGHT command.) The default value is usually a good guide by which to go.
Reflection	Use a higher value to create a shiny effect.
Roughness	This option relates to the reflection value. You set only the value — no color. A higher roughness setting produces a bigger reflection highlight.

Transparency	Set this option at the highest value to create a material that is completely transparent. A middle value creates a translucent material.
Refraction	Use refraction only in the Photo Raytrace renderer when you have a transparent (or translucent) material. Refraction is the bending of a light wave when it passes through an object. A higher value increases the refraction.
Bump Map	Bump maps make your material look bumpy. You use the bottom part of the dialog box to choose the bump map and for bump map settings.

Instead of creating a material from scratch, click Modify to change an existing material.

Or click Duplicate to make a copy of a material and then modify it. The New Standard Material dialog box (or one just like it) opens. Type a new name and make any changes you want.

To see the results, choose Sphere or Cube from the drop-down box under the Preview button. Then click Preview. Continue to fool around with the controls until you like what you see; then click OK to return to the Materials dialog box.

Attaching a material

Now comes the important part: Attaching your new material to an object. Choose your new material from the Materials list and click Attach. Back at your drawing, you can select an object.

You also can attach materials by clicking ACI (AutoCAD Color Index), which opens the (take a deep breath) Attach by AutoCAD Color Index dialog box, where you select a material and an ACI color. Preview displays the selected material. Attach attaches the selected material to the color. Detach detaches the selected material from its color.

Finally, you can attach materials by layer. Click By Layer to open the Attach by Layer dialog box, which works the same way as the Attach by AutoCAD Color Index dialog box.

Suppose that you want to attach a material that you created a while ago and you've forgotten its name, but know that you attached it to another object. Click the Select button, and pick the object in your drawing. AutoCAD returns you to the Materials dialog box, with the material selected.

Choose Detach to detach a material from an object.

ROTATE3D

More Stuff
See also the RENDER and MATLIB commands.

ROTATE

Rotates objects around a point.

 Toolbar: On the Modify toolbar, click the Rotate button.

Menu: Choose Modify⇨Rotate.

How to Use It
The default way to rotate objects is the simplest. Select an object. Specify a base point around which the object rotates. Type a rotation angle (this angle is relative to the object's current position). You also can pick a point to indicate the angle. Move the cursor, and the drag copy of the object moves.

You also can type **r** for the Reference option, which prompts you for a reference angle and a new angle. You can use this method to specify an absolute rotation and to align an object with other objects in your drawing.

ROTATE3D

Rotates objects in 3D space about an axis.

Menu: Choose Modify⇨3D Operation⇨Rotate 3D.

How to Use It
Before you start this command, you want to have in mind the axis for rotation. It may help to draw a line so that you can select it.

First, select the objects that you want to rotate. Next, the command offers you several options for defining the rotation axis:

2points	Specify two points on the axis.
Axis by object	Selects a line, circle, arc, or 2D polyline segment. If you select a line or a straight polyline segment, the selected object becomes the axis. If you pick a circle, arc, or arc polyline segment, an imaginary line going through the object's center and exiting it perpendicularly becomes the axis.
Last	Uses the preceding axis of rotation.
View	Aligns the axis with the viewing direction and passing through a point that you select.

| X, Y, or Z axis | Aligns the axis with the X, Y, or Z axis and passes through a point that you select. |

After you define your axis (didn't I tell you that it would be easiest to draw a line and select it?), type the rotation angle, or use the Reference option to specify a reference angle and a new angle as you would for the ROTATE command.

RPREF

Sets preferences for rendering.

Toolbar: On the Render toolbar, click the Rendering Preferences button.

Menu: Choose View➪Render➪Preferences.

How to Use It

This command opens the Rendering Preferences dialog box. This box is exactly the same as the Render dialog box. (See the RENDER command.) You can use this dialog box to set defaults for rendering. However, remember that you can change any setting in the Render dialog box at rendering time.

When you finish with your preferences, click OK, and go render!

RULESURF

Draws a ruled surface mesh between two objects.

Toolbar: On the Surfaces toolbar, click the Ruled Surface button.

Menu: Choose Draw➪Surfaces➪Ruled Surface.

How to Use It

Before you use this command, you need to draw two objects that will define the shape of the mesh. You can use points, lines, circles, arcs, or polylines. Both objects can be open or closed. AutoCAD prompts you to select the two defining curves (even though they can be straight). Then AutoCAD creates the surface.

More Stuff

If the objects are open, such as lines, where you pick the objects matters. If the pick points are on the same side of the two objects, the ruled lines start from the side where you picked and go straight across. If the pick points are on opposite sides of the two objects, the ruled lines cross from one end of the first object to the other end of the second object, creating a self-intersecting mesh. (Well, you have to try it.)

SAVE

Saves the drawing.

Command line only

How to Use It

Actually, this command has pretty much been superseded by QSAVE, which is available on the Standard toolbar and the File menu.

SAVEAS

Saves a drawing under a new or different name or in a different format.

Menu: Choose File⇨Save As.

How to Use It

This command opens the Save Drawing As dialog box. Type a new or different name in the File name text box. You can also use the Save as type drop-down list to save the drawing in Release 13/LT 95 or Release 12/LT 2 format. You can also save the file as a template.

More Stuff

See "Creating Terrific Templates" in Chapter 4 of *AutoCAD Release 14 For Dummies*.

SAVEIMG

Saves a rendered image to a file.

Menu: Choose Tools⇨Display Image⇨Save.

How to Use It

AutoCAD opens the Save Image dialog box.

134 SAVEURL

Select the type of file that you want to create. Your choices are .BMP, TGA, and TIFF. If you chose TGA or TIFF, click Options if you want to specify compression options.

In the Portion box, you can specify a portion of the image to save. Pick the lower-left and upper-right points. The result are reflected in the Offset and Size boxes. Offset is the X and Y distance (in pixels) from the lower-left corner of the Portion box. Size is the X and Y pixels of the area that you selected.

A handy Reset button enables you to reset the image to its original state.

More Stuff

If you've rendered to a Render Window, you can choose File⇨Save from the Render Window's menu. This command saves the rendering in the BMP format.

SAVEURL

See INTERNET UTILITIES.

SCALE

Changes the size of objects.

Toolbar: On the Modify toolbar, click the Scale button.

Menu: Choose Modify⇨Scale.

How to Use It

AutoCAD prompts you to select objects. Then you specify a base point; the object is scaled from that point. Next, type a scale factor. A factor of 2 doubles the size of the object; a factor of .25 reduces the object to one-quarter size.

You also can use the Reference option by typing **r** after you specify a base point. Specify a reference length and a new length.

SCENE

Creates, changes, and deletes *scenes*, which are like views but can have lighting effects. They're used for rendering.

Toolbar: On the Render toolbar, click the Scenes button.

Menu: Choose View⇨Render⇨Scene.

How to Use It

Before using this command, you usually use DDVIEW to create a view and the LIGHT command to add lights to a drawing. The SCENE command puts a view and lights together and names them so that you can use them for rendering.

AutoCAD opens the Scenes dialog box, which simply lists defined scenes. The dialog box has three options: New, Modify, and Delete.

New	Opens the New Scene dialog box to create a new scene. Under Scene Name, type a new name. The Views section lists views. Select a view or *CURRENT* from the list. Under Lights, select as many lights as you want or *ALL*.
Modify	Select one of the scenes from the Scenes dialog box, and click Modify. The Modify Scene dialog box opens. You can change the scene name, view, and lights.
Delete	Select one of the scenes from the Scenes dialog box, and click Delete. At the prompt, click OK to confirm the deletion.

More Stuff

Would you believe that you can have up to 500 lights in a scene? Talk about blinding!

SECTION

Creates a region from the intersection of a plane and solids. This region is the cross section of the solid.

 Toolbar: On the Solids toolbar, click the Section button.

Menu: Choose Draw➪Solids➪Section.

How to Use It

First, you need a solid to select. You also can have an object to select for the intersecting plane, or you can specify the plane during the command.

AutoCAD prompts you to select objects. If you select more than one solid, you get more than one region. Then choose options for defining the intersecting plane:

3points	Specify three points in the plane.
Object	Select a circle, ellipse, arc, 2D spline, or 2D polyline segment.

136 SELECT

Zaxis	First, specify a point on the plane; then specify a point on the Z axis of the plane, which means a point exiting the plane perpendicularly. This vector is called a *normal*.
View	Specify a point in the view plane.
XY, YZ, ZX or ZX plane	These options align the sectioning plane with the XY, YZ, or ZX plane. You simply pick a point in the plane.

SELECT

Puts selected objects in the Previous selection set so that you can use the set with the next command.

Command line only

How to Use It

You select objects with the SELECT command just as you do for any other command that asks you to select objects. Here, for the record, is the complete, exhaustive list of the ways you can select objects. After you select the objects, press Enter to complete the command; then you start any editing command. Type **p** (for previous) to select all the objects.

AUto	This option is the default, so you probably are using it without knowing. The option simply means that pointing to an object selects it and that pointing to a blank space starts the first corner of a window, regular (see Window) or crossing.
Add	This option, also the default, means that you can add objects to the selection set by selecting them so that you get more and more objects.
ALL	Selects all objects in the drawing except ones on frozen or locked layers.
BOX	This option means that you select two diagonal points that define a box. If the first point you select is on the left and the second is on the right, this option is the same as Window. If you pick points from right to left, this option is the same as Crossing. Auto includes this option.
Crossing	You select two diagonal points that define a box or window, starting from the right and ending on the left. Any objects inside the box or crossing its perimeter are selected.

SELECTURL

CPolygon	This option is like Crossing, but instead of picking two points, you pick a whole bunch of them, in a sort of roundabout direction, to create a polygon. Any objects inside the box or crossing its perimeter are selected.
Fence	This option is like CPolygon, but open — a bunch of continuous lines that select any object they cross.
Group	Selects objects in a named group. You have to type the name. (See the GROUP command.)
Last	Selects the most recently created object.
Multiple	This option enables you to select objects without highlighting them during the selection process.
Previous	Selects the same objects that were selected in the last selection process. The SELECT command uses this option. The Previous option enables you to use several commands on the same set of objects. The Previous selection set gets lost if you erase objects or switch between paper and model space.
Remove	Use this option and everything you select is removed from the selection set instead of added. (This situation can get confusing.) Use the Add option when you finish removing and want to start adding.
SIngle	This option is for selecting only one object. AutoCAD doesn't prompt you to select any more objects.
Undo	Cancels the most recent selection.
Window	You pick two points, from left to right; everything that's completely inside the box's perimeter is selected.
WPolygon	This option is the same as CPolygon, except that only objects completely inside the polygon are selected.

More Stuff

"Selecting objects with the SELECT command" section in Chapter 7 of *AutoCAD Release 14 For Dummies* discusses this command in detail.

SELECTURL

See INTERNET UTILITIES.

'SETVAR

Sets values for system variables.

Menu: Choose Tools⇨Inquiry⇨Set Variable.

How to Use It

System variables store all sorts of information about your drawing and about AutoCAD in general. Usually, you can use a regular command. When you use DDIM to create a dimension style, for example, you affect a whole slew of system variables that relate to dimensions.

Occasionally, you may need to change a system variable directly. If you know the variable's name, you don't even need the SETVAR command. Type the variable name and press Enter; then type the new value and press Enter to end the command.

You can get a list of all the variables by typing **?** at the first prompt.

More Stuff

See Part III of this book for a list of system variables not accessible by regular commands.

SHADE

Creates a shaded image 3D object. Shading is much simpler than rendering.

Toolbar: On the Render toolbar, click the Shade button.

Menu: Choose View⇨Shade.

How to Use It

When you use this command, AutoCAD shades everything in the current viewport, based on one light source.

More Stuff

If your screen shows fewer than 256 colors, SHADE doesn't include a lighting effect.

See also the SHADEDGE system variable in Part III under "3D."

SKETCH

Draws freehand line segments.

Command line only

How to Use It

This command is for you artists out there. When you start the command, AutoCAD prompts you for a *record increment* — the length of the line segments. The smaller the increment, the smoother the line. SKETCH draws temporary lines and adds them permanently when you exit. This command gives you a little menu that contains the following options:

Pen	Typing **p** raises and lowers the imaginary sketching pen. When the pen is lowered, you can sketch. Raise the pen to stop sketching.
eXit	Exits sketch mode and gives you a report on how many lines you sketched.
Quit	Erases all the temporary lines. You use this option a lot, because it's darn hard to get anything to look good with this command. So quit and try again.
Record	Makes the temporary lines permanent and gives you a report on the number of lines recorded.
Erase	Erases any portion of a temporary line and raises the pen (if it is down).
Connect	Lowers the pen to continue sketching from the end of the last sketched line.
. (period)	Lowers the pen, draws a straight line from the end of the last sketched line to your current position, and raises the pen again. (You have to see this to understand it.)

More Stuff

You won't use this command often, but it's fun. You can use the command when you want to draw squiggly lines — in a map, for example. (Remember Etch-a-Sketch?)

SLICE

Slices a solid with a plane. You can retain one or both sides of the sliced solid.

 Toolbar: On the Solids toolbar, click the Slice button.

Menu: Choose Draw⇨Solids⇨Slice.

'SNAP

How to Use It

First, you need a solid object to slice. You also may want to have some object that you can select to define the slicing plane.

Select the solid. Then specify the plane by using one of the following methods:

3points	Specify three points in the plane.
Object	Select a circle, ellipse, arc, 2D spline, or 2D polyline segment.
Zaxis	First, specify a point in the plane; then specify a point on the Z axis of the plane, which means a point that exits the plane perpendicularly. This is called a *normal*.
View	Specify a point in the view plane.
XY, YZ, ZX	Aligns the sectioning plane with the XY, YZ, or ZX plane. You just pick a point in the plane.

AutoCAD then prompts you for a point on the desired side of the plane. If you pick a point, the part of the solid on that side of the plane is retained. The rest of the solid goes poof! Type **b** to keep both sides.

'SNAP

Snaps the cursor to set intervals on an imaginary grid. This command is used for drawing to exact points.

Command line only to set the interval

To turn SNAP on and off, double-click SNAP in the status bar. On most systems, you can also use F9 or Ctrl+B.

How to Use It

The shortcut methods in the preceding section only turn snap on or off, using the current value for snap spacing. To change the snap spacing, rotation, and style, use the DDRMODES command or SNAP command at the command line. For snap spacing, just type a number. Typing **.25**, for example, makes the cursor jump to every quarter-unit.

Use the Aspect option when you want the X and Y spacing to be different. Rotation rotates the crosshairs and snap points from a base point. Specify the base point and rotation angle. Style enables you to change to isometric mode. (See the ISOPLANE command.)

SOLID

Draws filled 2D polygons.

 Toolbar: On the Surfaces toolbar, click the Solid button.

Menu: Choose Draw⇨Surfaces⇨2D Solid.

How to Use It

First, use the FILL command to turn fill on. SOLID prompts you to specify two points. Now comes the tricky part. At the prompt for the third point, pick a point diagonally opposite the second point that you picked (this is *not* ring-around-a-rosy). If you want a triangle, press Enter at the prompt for a fourth point.

If you want more than three sides, pick a fourth point diagonally opposite from your first point. Again, you can end here by pressing Enter, but AutoCAD keeps prompting you for third and fourth points so that you can expand your polygon in new and unusual shapes.

More Stuff

Picking points around a rosy — that is, around the perimeter of your polygon — results in the infamous AutoCAD bow tie that all of us have created too many times in the past. Try it, and join the family of frustrated AutoCAD users!

'SPELL

Checks the spelling of text.

 Toolbar: On the Standard toolbar, click the Spelling button.

Menu: Choose Tools⇨Spelling.

How to Use It

Select the text that you want to spell check. The text can be created with TEXT, DTEXT, or MTEXT. AutoCAD opens the Check Spelling dialog box. As AutoCAD finds a misspelled word, it displays the word in the Current word box and suggests alternatives in the Suggestions box. The Context box shows you the phrase in which the misspelled word was found. Here are the options:

 **SPHERE**

Ignore	Leaves that occurrence of the word alone and goes on to the next.
Ignore All	Ignores all occurrences of the word.
Change	Changes that occurrence of the word to whatever is in the Suggestions box.
Change All	Changes all occurrences of the word to whatever is in the Suggestions box.
Add	Adds the word to the current dictionary.
Lookup	Checks the spelling of the word in the Suggestions box.

You also can change dictionaries.

More Stuff

See "Checking It Out" in Chapter 9 of *AutoCAD Release 14 For Dummies*.

SPHERE

Draws a 3D solid sphere.

 Toolbar: On the Solids toolbar, click the Sphere button.

Menu: Choose Draw⇨Solids⇨Sphere.

How to Use It

If you're looking for a smooth entry into 3D, you're in the right place. AutoCAD makes drawing spheres easy.

First, specify a 3D point for the center of the sphere (X,Y,Z coordinates). Then specify a length for the radius or type **d** to specify a diameter.

SPLINE

Draws a spline curve. A spline uses a series of points as a frame to create a smooth curve.

 Toolbar: On the Draw toolbar, click the Spline button.

Menu: Choose Draw⇨Spline.

How to Use It

Specify two to seven points to define the polyline. Press Enter when you finish picking points. Although the prompt doesn't tell you, you can type **undo** after any point to remove it — another example of AutoCAD's clear, user-friendly interface.

The SPLINE command now demands that you enter start and end tangent points to define the angle of the start and end of the spline. (No, I'm not going to give you a course in geometry here.) Move the cursor to see the result on the curve. You can press Enter and have AutoCAD calculate default tangents.

You can type **c** to close the spline. You can choose the Fit Tolerance option and enter a value in units. A 0 tolerance means that the spline has to go through each point; a bigger number gives the spline more leeway, resulting in a less accurate but smoother curve.

More Stuff

At the first prompt, you also can choose the Object option. Then pick the 2D or 3D polyline on which you used the Spline option. SPLINE converts the polyline to a spline and deletes the polylines.

For your information, the technical name for what SPLINE draws is a quadratic or cubic Nonuniform rational B-spline (or NURBS) curve. Sounds NURBY to me.

SPLINEDIT

Edits splines.

Toolbar: On the Modify II toolbar, click the Edit Spline button.

Menu: Choose Modify➪Object➪Spline.

How to Use It

In order to understand editing splines, you need to understand control points and fit points:

- ✦ Fit points are the points you picked when you created the spline.

- ✦ Control points are points that AutoCAD determines mathematically to display the spline.

Now, select the spline. The control points are shown as grips. Notice that they're not on the spline. Here are your options:

SPLINEDIT

Fit Data		This shows your fit points which are on the spline unless you specified a tolerance greater than 0. This option doesn't appear if you purged the fit data (how dare you?), refined the spline, or use the Tolerance and Close or Open options together, or move a control point. If the option appears and you choose it, the grips now show the fit points instead of the control points and you get the following submenu:
	Add	Adds fit points to a spline. You select a fit point and then a new point. The new point goes between the selected point and the next point.
	Close	Closes the spline.
	Open	Opens a closed spline.
	Delete	Deletes a selected fit point.
	Move	Moves fit points. You get a sub-submenu (are you following me?) that enables you to move to the next or preceding point, select a point, exit the sub-submenu (whew!), or pick a new location for the fit point that you selected.
	Purge	Removes the spline's fit data from the drawing database. AutoCAD can create the spline with only the control points.
	Tangents	Specifies new start and end tangents. (See the SPLINE command.)
	toLerance	Type **L** to get this option, which sets a new tolerance. (See the SPLINE command.)
	eXit	Leaves the submenu and returns to the original prompt.
Close		Same as Close in the submenu.
Open		Same as Open in the submenu.
Move Vertex		Oh no, another submenu. The Next and Previous options enable you to move from vertex to vertex. After you have it, pick the new location. Alternatively, you can choose Select Point to pick the vertex you want to move and then pick its new location. Of course, you also have the eXit option (thank goodness).
Refine		This command offers you suboptions so that you can add control points, elevate the spline's order (the words are so obscure that I can't even think of a joke about them, but they mean allowing for more control points — I suppose that makes the spline more orderly), and give more weight to certain control points, which is sort of like increasing their gravitational pull on the spline.
rEverse		Reverses the spline's direction.
Undo		Cancels the last editing operation. (You need this option often, I assure you.)
eXit		Ends the SPLINEDIT command.

STATS

Lists rendering information.

Toolbar: On the Render toolbar, click the Statistics button.

Menu: Choose View⇨Render⇨Statistics.

How to Use It

This command provides the following information:

- ✦ Scene Name
- ✦ Last Rendering Type
- ✦ Rendering Time for the last rendering
- ✦ Total Faces processed during the last rendering
- ✦ Total Triangles processed during the last rendering

This command is just an opportunity for AutoCAD to brag about how complicated rendering really is. Click Save Statistics to File and type a filename if you want to save the information to a file. You can type an existing filename, and AutoCAD appends the information, giving you a running log of all your renderings.

'STATUS

Lists the status of drawing statistics and modes.

Menu: Choose Tools⇨Inquiry⇨Status.

How to Use It

This command lists the status of many of the commands you use for setting up your drawing, the current layer, color, and linetype, and some system-wide information such as free disk space, memory, and swap file space.

STRETCH

Stretches objects.

Toolbar: On the Modify toolbar, click the Stretch button.

Menu: Choose Modify⇨Stretch.

'STYLE

How to Use It

AutoCAD prompts you to select objects. You *must* use the crossing window or CPolygon method of selection. Any line, arc, or polyline that *crosses* the selection window is stretched by moving the endpoints that lie *inside* the window. Enclose the endpoints of the objects that you want stretched in the crossing window, and you come out okay. Objects completely inside the window are just moved.

Like the MOVE command, STRETCH asks you for a base point and a second point of displacement.

'STYLE

Creates text styles.

Menu: Choose Format⇨Text Style.

How to Use It

AutoCAD opens the Text Style dialog box. In the Style Name section, choose a style from the drop-down list to make that style current. You can also delete or rename a style. To create a new style, click New and name the new style. Click OK. To modify an existing style, choose it from the list.

Use the rest of the dialog box to define a new or redefine an existing style.

In the Font section, choose a font, a style (such as bold or italic) if it's supported by the font you chose and then set a height. If you set the height to 0, AutoCAD prompts you for the height each time you use it and you can vary the height if you wish.

In the Effects section, choose Backwards, Upside-down, and Vertical if you want those effects. The Vertical option (like text going down the spine of a book) appears only for certain fonts that support it.

Now specify a width factor. A value of 1 is normal. A larger number gives you fat text; a smaller number (between 0 and 1) gives you skinny text.

For the obliquing angle, type an angle. Angles between 0 and 85 result in italics.

The Preview box shows you the beautiful style that you've created. Use the Preview text box to type whatever you want. Click Preview and AutoCAD shows you that text in the Preview box.

Click Apply to apply the style to all text in your drawing that uses that style. Then click Close to close the dialog box.

Release 14 supports all the TrueType fonts that you've installed on your computer.

More Stuff

AutoCAD comes with one style, called STANDARD. This style is boring, so create your own. All the text commands offer you an opportunity to change the style before you start writing your novel.

See the section "Creating Text styles" in Chapter 9 of *AutoCAD Release 14 For Dummies*.

SUBTRACT

Subtracts the area of one region, or the volume of one solid, from another.

Toolbar: On the Modify II toolbar, click the Subtract button.

Menu: Choose Modify⇨Boolean⇨Subtract.

How to Use It

First, select the regions or solids you want to subtract from; then select the objects you want to subtract. AutoCAD does the rest.

TABLET

Calibrates a tablet with a paper drawing that you want to digitize. Also configures the tablet menu.

Menu: Choose Tools⇨Tablet.

How to Use It

Use this command if you use a digitizer.

The CFG option

The first time you use your digitizing tablet, use the CFG option to configure the menu and screen pointing areas (where you draw) of a large tablet. The menu should be attached to the tablet surface — either the one that AutoCAD provides (look for Acadr14\Sample\ tablet14.dwg) or your own customized one.

148 TABLET

AutoCAD prompts you for the number of tablet menus you want. The menu is divided into areas; you type the number of areas that you're using. If you want to realign the tablet menu areas, type **y** at the next prompt. You need to digitize the points requested for each area. Then AutoCAD asks you how many columns and rows you want for each menu area. In this way, AutoCAD divides each menu area into little boxes, one for each command.

Finally, AutoCAD asks whether you want to respecify the screen pointing area — that's the big box in the middle of the tablet drawing which represents where you draw. Type **y** if you do and digitize the points as requested.

The CAL option

To digitize a paper drawing, first tape the drawing neatly and securely to the digitizer tablet. Then mark three or more points on the paper — perhaps the corners. You can set the lower-left corner as 0,0. Then measure the other points, and write in their coordinates relative to 0,0. If the drawing represents something big like a building, use real-life coordinates. You'll need these coordinates later.

Use the CAL option to calibrate the tablet area with your drawing. Then use the ON option to turn the tablet on. When you finish, turn the tablet off to return to regular drawing mode.

To calibrate the tablet area, type **CAL**; AutoCAD displays the prompt digitize point #1. With your puck or stylus, pick one of the points that you marked on the paper. AutoCAD prompts you for the point's coordinates. (I told you that you'd need those coordinates.) AutoCAD keeps prompting you for points and their coordinates. You can enter as many points as you want.

Depending on how many points you entered, AutoCAD may provide a very esoteric table that relates to various types of transformations, called Orthogonal, Affine, and Projective. You have to choose, so try Orthogonal. If you don't like the result, I refer you to the AutoCAD command reference documentation. (This information is not the stuff of a Quick Reference.)

ON and OFF

Use the ON and OFF options to turn the tablet on and off. When the tablet is on, the entire digitizer can be used for digitizing a drawing. When the tablet is off, you use just the small drawing area to draw and the rest for menus. You can usually press Ctrl+T to toggle the tablet on and off.

TABSURF

Draws a 3D tabulated surface, based on a curve and a direction (called a *vector*).

 Toolbar: On the Surfaces toolbar, click the Tabulated Surface button.

Menu: Choose Draw➪Surfaces➪Tabulated Surface.

How to Use It

You need to select the *path curve*, which defines the shape of the surface, and a *direction vector*, which specifies the direction in which the shape will be extruded. Draw these objects before using the command.

AutoCAD prompts you for a path curve and direction vector. You select objects for each of these items. The path curve can be a line, arc, circle, ellipse, polyline, or spline. The direction vector must be a line or an open polyline. AutoCAD creates the surface.

More Stuff

For the direction vector, AutoCAD ignores any intermediate meandering; it simply considers the beginning and end points. The results of this command are somewhat like those of the EXTRUDE command, except that this command creates a surface and the EXTRUDE command creates a solid.

TEXT

Creates a line of text. This command has been superseded, in my opinion, by DTEXT, so I refer you there. However, TEXT is still used when customizing AutoCAD in script files and AutoLISP routines.

'TIME

Lists date and time information for a drawing.

Menu: Choose Tools➪Inquiry➪Time.

How to Use It

The TIME command displays when the drawing was created and last updated. This command also tracks the total editing time minus plotting time (not including time when you worked, but didn't save your changes). In addition, you can turn a timer on and off for more customized timing. (Maybe you don't want to charge a customer for correcting a mistake that was your fault.) To turn on the timer, use the ON option; to turn it off, use the OFF option. Reset brings the timer back to 0.

More Stuff

The timer is on by default, so AutoCAD is always timing you!

TOLERANCE

Creates geometric tolerances.

 Toolbar: On the Dimension toolbar, click the Tolerance button.

Menu: Choose Dimension➪Tolerance.

How to Use It

To use this command, you have to understand tolerances. (I'm not about to give you a lesson on the topic here, but briefly, a tolerance specifies how much an actual manufactured object can deviate from an exact measurement.) AutoCAD creates *feature control frames*, which are little boxes that contain the tolerance information that you choose to put there. The frames are then placed next to your dimensions.

TOLERANCE first opens the Symbol dialog box. Click the type of tolerance symbol that you want. Click Help to get a list of what each symbol means. Click OK after you're done.

Up pops the Geometric Tolerance dialog box, in which you build your feature control frame. This dialog box allows for up to two lines of symbols. You build a line from left to right, as follows:

Sym	This is the first column, containing the symbol you chose in the Symbol dialog box.
Tolerance 1	If you want to start with the diameter symbol, click the Dia box. Then type the tolerance value in the Value box. Click the MC box to open the Material Condition dialog box. These symbols define conditions that apply to materials that can vary in size. M is for At maximum material condition, L is for At least material condition, and S means Regardless of feature size. Click the option you want and then click OK to return to the Geometric Tolerance dialog box.
Tolerance 2	If you want a second tolerance, create it just as you did the first.

TOOLBAR

Datum 1	*Datum* refers to a theoretically exact geometrical entity from which you can verify the dimensions of your objects. First, type a reference letter that represents your first datum. Click MC if you want to insert a material condition. This process is the same one used in creating the tolerance.
Datum 2	Same procedure as Datum 1.
Datum 3	Same procedure as Datum 1.
Projected Tolerance Zone	Type a height, and click the Projected Tolerance Zone box to put in the Projected Tolerance Zone symbol.

The dialog box disappears, and AutoCAD prompts you for the tolerance location. Pick a point and AutoCAD inserts it.

TOOLBAR

Shows, hides, and customizes toolbars.

Toolbar: Right-click any toolbar.

Menu: Choose View➪Toolbars.

How to Use It

AutoCAD opens the Toolbars dialog box.

Managing toolbars

To show a toolbar, click the name of the toolbar that you want to show. Then click Close. To hide a toolbar, uncheck it. You also can select a toolbar and delete it. The Show ToolTips button controls whether the button name appears when you place the mouse on the button. Unless you have memorized all the buttons, keep this option checked! You can click Large Buttons if the standard ones are too itsy-bitsy for you, but of course, they take up much more of your screen.

You don't need the TOOLBARS command to hide toolbars. To hide a *floating* toolbar (one that floats somewhere in the drawing area and is not *docked* on the edges of the screen), click the Close button in the upper-right corner. If the toolbar is docked, you can use a simple (and undocumented) method to hide it — drag it from its border onto the drawing area to float it and then click the Close button.

The only things left to know are how to dock a floating toolbar and how to float a docked one. These terms may be making you seasick, but you soon see that setting up your drawing space for your ease and comfort is worthwhile.

To dock a floating toolbar, click the toolbar name and then drag the toolbar to the top, bottom, left side, or right side of the screen. The toolbar changes to fit its new location.

To float a docked toolbar, click the gray border around its edge and then drag the toolbar to the drawing area. You can drag the edges of floating toolbars to morph them into any shape.

Creating a new toolbar

Creating a new toolbar that contains the commands you use most and the ones that are hardest to get to is a great idea. However, use AutoCAD for a while before you do so, keeping a wish list of commands that you wish were more accessible. These commands are the ones that you want to put in your new toolbar. From the Toolbars dialog box, click New. Type a toolbar name and menu group. (The menu group is ACAD, unless you've created a custom menu, in which case its name appears.) Then click OK. An empty toolbar of your own creation appears on-screen. Now click Customize to add buttons to your toolbar. Click Categories, and the buttons for that category appear, helping you find the button that you want. Drag the button from the dialog box to your new toolbar. You also can copy a button from another toolbar by holding down the Ctrl key while you drag the button to the new toolbar. In addition, you can drag an icon to an existing toolbar.

You can only drag buttons while the Customize Toolbars dialog box is open.

More Stuff

There's more, lots more. You can use the Button Editor to design your own buttons; you can create flyouts, too.

TORUS

Draws a 3D donut.

Toolbar: On the Solids toolbar, click the Torus button.

Menu: Choose Draw⇨Solids⇨Torus.

How to Use It

First, specify the center with a 3D point. Then type a value for the radius of the torus, that is, the distance from the center to the outside of the torus. Next, type a value for the radius of the tube, which is half the width of the tube. At each radius prompt, you also can type **d** and then specify a diameter.

TRACE

Draws lines that can have a width.

This command has been superseded by the PLINE command.

TRANSPARENCY

Enables you to create transparent images for image types that support transparent pixels.

Toolbar: On the Reference toolbar, click the Image Transparency button.

Menu: Choose Modify⇨Object⇨Image⇨Transparency.

How to Use It

Select an image object and type **on** or **off**. The default is off.

More Stuff

Not all images support transparency.

TRIM

Trims objects at an edge created by another object.

Toolbar: On the Modify toolbar, click the Trim button.

Menu: Choose Modify⇨Trim.

How to Use It

First, select the cutting edge. (You can select more than one edge.) The object that you want to trim will be cut off where it intersects that edge (or those edges). You also can trim the object to where it *would* intersect the cutting edge, if the cutting edge were extended (called an *implied intersection*).

Now select the object to be trimmed. Pay attention — you have to select on the part of object that you want to trim. If you've selected two edges and want the object to be trimmed between then, select the object between the edges. The result is like the BREAK command.

If the edge has only an implied intersection with your object, use the Edge option and then turn on the Extend option before selecting your object. That way, AutoCAD knows to calculate the implied intersection. Be sure to select the object on the side you want to trim.

More Stuff

Trimming in 3D is a bit more complicated, as you may expect. Select the cutting edge and then type **p** (for projection). You have three projection choices:

None	Trims objects that intersect with the cutting edge in true 3D (you know — real life on your computer screen).
Ucs	Projects on the XY plane of the current User Coordinate System (UCS).
View	Projects along the current view plane.

You can use the Edge option for 3D trimming as well.

U

Undoes the last operation.

Toolbar: On the Standard toolbar, click the Undo button.

Menu: Choose Edit⇨Undo.

How to Use It

U is one of the nicest, sweetest commands around; you could hug it. Amazingly, you can use this command over and over; AutoCAD undoes every (well, almost every) command until you get to where you were at the beginning of the drawing session. Now *that's* a database. Obviously, U cannot undo things such as plotting or saving your drawing.

More Stuff

See also the UNDO command, which is a more robust version of U.

UCS

Manages the User Coordinate System (UCS).

Toolbar: On the Standard toolbar, click the UCS button.

Menu: Choose Tools⇨UCS.

How to Use It

UCS has the following options most of which enable you to define the origin of the new UCS and the direction of the axes.

Origin	Changes the origin, leaving the axes in the same direction as before.
Zaxis	You define an origin and a point on the positive Z axis. The XY axis is tilted accordingly.
3point	The first point is the origin. Then specify any point on the desired X axis. Finally, specify a point on the new Y axis.
OBject	Results depend on the object. For example, if you pick a point on the circumference of a circle, the origin is the circle's center and the X axis passes through your pick point.
View	Creates a new UCS with the XY plane parallel to your current viewpoint (that is, parallel to your screen). The origin remains unchanged. This option is a good for creating text that looks normal on a 3D drawing viewed at an angle. It's not good for much else.
X	Rotates the UCS around the X axis. You specify the rotation angle. The origin remains unchanged.
Y	Rotates the UCS around the Y axis. You specify the rotation angle. The origin remains unchanged.
Z	Rotates the UCS around the Z axis. You specify the rotation angle. The origin remains unchanged. This option can be used in 2D drawings.
Prev	Brings back the previous UCS.
Restore	Brings back a saved UCS.
Save	Saves a UCS. You get to give it a name of up to 31 characters (no spaces allowed). Word to the wise — save all useful UCSs.
Del	Deletes a saved UCS.
?	Lists all your UCSs and their properties.
World	Returns you to the familiar World Coordinate System.

More Stuff

A UCS sets the direction of the X,Y,Z coordinates. Setting the viewpoint is a separate process, which you perform with DDVPOINT or VPOINT. If you restore a UCS and don't understand why you're looking at things from such a strange angle, use the PLAN command to return to the plan view of the UCS.

See Part I, Creating a User Coordinate System (UCS). ***See also*** the UCSFOLLOW system variable in Part III under "3D."

UCSICON

Manages the UCS icon itself (which usually appears in the lower-left corner of your screen). This command doesn't affect the UCS.

Menu: Choose View⇨Display⇨UCS Icon.

How to Use It

The ON option displays the UCS icon; OFF turns it off. Noorigin (no, that's not Norwegian) shows the icon at the lower-left corner of your screen or viewport, no matter where the UCS origin is. The Origin option forces the icon to appear at the origin of the UCS, if there's room.

UNDO

Undoes commands.

Command line only

How to Use It

This command is the big brother or sister (are commands masculine or feminine?) of the U command. Amazingly, AutoCAD retains a database of every action performed during a drawing session so that you can undo commands and return to the pristine state in which you started. Following are the options:

Number	This option is the default. Type a number, and AutoCAD reverses the effect of that many commands. The difference between using this option and using U five times is simply that this option doesn't cause regeneration between each undoing. (Using U five times may or may not cause regeneration, depending on the commands.)
Auto	Undoes any operation performed with a menu used as one command.
Control	This option displays a submenu, which contains the options that control the way UNDO works. The All option gives you the full UNDO command. None turns off the U and UNDO commands. (Be careful — being able to undo commands is always nice.) One limits UNDO to reversing one command.
BEgin	This option groups a series of commands. Use this option when you're trying something new and exciting (but a little dangerous) and you want to be able to undo your work in one fell swoop. Then use U or UNDO 1 to undo the entire group.

'VIEW

End	Ends the group started by BEgin.
Mark	Places a mark at the current location. You then use the Back option to undo back to the mark.
Back	This option can be dangerous. You use Back to undo commands back to the most recent mark. But if you haven't created any marks, watch out. Luckily, AutoCAD displays this prompt: This will undo everything. OK? Quickly type **n** — unless you want to undo everything that you've done today!

More Stuff

Obviously, some commands can't be undone. If you used the LIST command to get information about an object, AutoCAD won't get inside your head and remove the knowledge you've gained. (That's not on my list for a new feature for AutoCAD 15, either!)

UNION

Creates one combined region or solid from two or more regions or solids.

Toolbar: On the Modify II toolbar, click the Union button.

Menu: Choose Modify⇨Boolean⇨Union.

How to Use It

This command is how two regions or solids join in holy matrimony (very unexciting, I assure you). First, select the objects. If the objects aren't regions or solids and can be converted, AutoCAD converts them. All you have to do is watch. (I told you, it's okay; nothing too risqué happens.)

'UNITS

See the DDUNITS command, which manages units from a dialog box.

'VIEW

See the DDVIEW command.

VIEWRES

Sets the resolution for circles and arcs, and controls Fast Zoom mode.

Command line only

How to Use It

AutoCAD first asks whether you want fast zooms. You almost always do.

Now comes the reason why you came to this command in the first place. AutoCAD asks you to enter a circle zoom percentage (1 to 20,000) and tells you the current setting. The higher the setting, the smoother your circles and arcs will be — and the slower AutoCAD's speed will be. Lower numbers speed things, but circles can look like polygons. Usually, you can get a setting that gives you smooth circles, and you won't notice the millisecond decrease in speed.

More Stuff

If you see a circle that looks like a polygon, don't always assume you have to change VIEWRES. Try a REGEN first.

VPLAYER

Freezes and thaws layers within floating viewports.

 Toolbar: On the Object Properties toolbar, click the Layers button.

How to Use It

First, turn TILEMODE off by double-clicking the TILE button in the status bar. Release 14 has introduced a new way of using the VPLAYER command using the Layer & Linetype Properties dialog box — which you can also access using the LAYER command.

The Layer & Linetype Properties dialog box lets you freeze and thaw layers in current and New floating viewports.

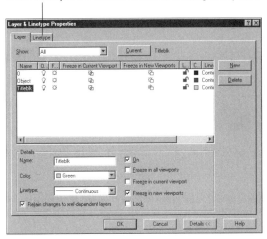

When you open this dialog box, all the columns are very narrow and you can't see the column headings. AutoCAD provides you with two solutions to this problem. Place the cursor over any heading and its title pops up as a ToolTip. You can also place the cursor on the bar that divides the columns and drag it to the right to widen the column. That's what I've done for the figure you see here.

To freeze a layer in the current (active) floating viewport, click its sun icon in the Freeze in Current Viewport column. The sun icon changes to a snowflake. To thaw it, click the snowflake icon.

To freeze a layer for new viewports that you're planning to create, click its sun icon in the Freeze in New Viewports column. To thaw a layer — you guessed it — click its snowflake icon.

Notice that you can also use the Details section to freeze and thaw layers for the current and new viewports. (The figure shows the Layer & Linetype Properties dialog box with its Details section displayed. Click Details at the bottom of the dialog box to show and hide this section.) Just select a layer and check or uncheck the item you want.

A simpler way to freeze or thaw a layer in the current (active) viewport is to click the Layer Control drop-down list on the Object Properties toolbar and click the icon for the layer in the Freeze/thaw in current viewport column — it's the third column.

VPOINT

More Stuff

You can't work with a layer that's frozen.

VPOINT

Controls the 3D angle from which you view your drawing.

Menu: Choose View⇨3D Viewpoint⇨Tripod.

How to Use It

The VPOINT command does the same thing as the DDVPOINT command, except that it offers a different conceptualization of 3D space with which to define your viewpoint.

Imagine making two, long, crossing cuts in the bottom of a tangerine. Open up the peel and lay it out flat on the table. AutoCAD uses a compass, shown in the figure, to represent the same concept. Just as the center of the tangerine peel was at the top of the tangerine, the center of the compass is the North Pole, equivalent to plan view (the familiar 2D way of looking at things from the top). As the outer edge of the peel was at the bottom of the tangerine, the outer ring is the South Pole. The whole Southern Hemisphere has been flattened out so that you can see it. The circle between the center and the outer ring is the equator. Anywhere you click inside the inner circle results in a view from above.

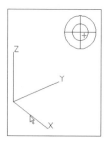

Anywhere you click between the inner and outer circles results in a view from below.

You also have to choose the corner of the Northern or Southern Hemisphere. You do this by paying attention to the crosshairs that go through the circles. Anything below the horizontal crosshair is a front view just as anything in the bottom half of the peel would have come from the front of the tangerine; anything above the horizontal crosshair is a back view. To the left of the vertical crosshair is a view from the left. To the right of the vertical crosshair is a view from the right. These front, back, left, and right directions are meaningful in relationship to the plan view. The Earth doesn't have a front, back, left, or right. But when you look at things from the top, you think that way.

Along with the compass you see a tripod. You pick your viewpoint on the compass and see the results on the tripod, which is just X,Y,Z axes moving in space. When you pick a point, AutoCAD returns you to your drawing, displaying the new viewpoint.

I hope that this explanation helps. Otherwise, create a model that doesn't look the same on all sides, start picking points, and see the results.

More Stuff

See also the UCS command for information on creating a User Coordinate System.

VPORTS

Creates tiled viewports.

Menu: Choose View⇨Tiled Viewports.

How to Use It

The TILE button on the status bar must be on to use this command. AutoCAD calls the number and layout of viewports *viewport configurations*. Choose Layout from the Tiled Viewports sub-menu to open the Tiled Viewport Layout dialog box. Here you can easily choose a configuration that suits your needs. You can create custom configurations by clicking a viewport to make it active and using VPORTS on that viewport. Use the Delete option to delete configurations. Join combines two adjacent viewports. Pick the *dominant* viewport first and then the secondary one. The new viewport has the zoom, viewpoint, and other features of the dominant one (which simply means that you picked it first).

When you have your viewports, use the Save option and give the configuration a name. Typing **?** lists other saved configurations. Use the Restore option to bring back saved configurations. (Bring back, Bring back, Oh bring back my viewports to me, to me. Do you think it'll make the Top 40?)

SIngle is your panic button for getting rid of all those unruly viewports and returning to one viewport, the default. The one viewport shows the view of the active viewport.

WBLOCK

If you're working in 3D, now is the time to use the DDVPOINT or VPOINT command to do something interesting with your viewports. Click anywhere inside a viewport to make it active, and create different views in each viewport. Even if you're working in 2D, viewports can show different parts of your drawing at different zooms. You can draw from one viewport to another. The possibilities are endless!

More Stuff

See the section, "Viewports in model space," in Chapter 15 of *AutoCAD Release 14 For Dummies*.

WBLOCK

Saves a block as a file on your hard disk. (WBLOCK stands for Write block.)

Command line only

How to Use It

AutoCAD opens the Create Drawing File dialog box. Type a name for the file and click Save. WBLOCK prompts you for a block name. You have four options:

- ✦ Type an equal sign (=). Do this when you want the file and block to have the same name. Then press Enter. WBLOCK saves the block as a file on your hard disk so that you can use it in other drawings.

- ✦ Press Enter. This option enables you to create a block and save it as a file in one command. WBLOCK displays all the usual BLOCK prompts. In this case, the objects that you selected are deleted. Use OOPS to restore the objects if you wish.

- ✦ Type the name of an existing block. AutoCAD writes that block to a drawing file. (You cannot enter the name of an external reference (xref) or one of its dependent blocks.)

- ✦ Type an asterisk (*). AutoCAD writes the entire drawing to a drawing file.

See also the BMAKE and OOPS commands for more information.

More Stuff

See the section "Rock and Block," in Chapter 14 of *AutoCAD Release 14 For Dummies* by Bud Smith, for a discussion on blocks.

WEDGE

Draws a 3D solid wedge.

Toolbar: On the Solids toolbar, click the Wedge button.

Menu: Choose Draw⇨Solids⇨Wedge.

How to Use It

At the prompt, specify a first corner for the base of your wedge. Then specify a diagonally opposite base corner. If the Z values of your points are different, AutoCAD uses the difference to create the height of the wedge. If the Z values are the same, AutoCAD prompts you for a height.

The cube option means a wedge with sides of equal length. You still specify the first point. Then type **c** (for cube) and type a length enabling you to define length, width, and height after specifying a first corner.

More Stuff

You can enter negative distances to draw the wedge in the direction of the negative axes.

XCLIP

Displays only the portion of an external reference inside a boundary and/or plane you specify.

Toolbar: On the Reference toolbar, click the External Reference Clip button.

Menu: Choose Modify⇨Object⇨Clip.

How to Use It

Select an xref. At the `ON/OFF/Clipdepth/Delete/generate Polyline/<New boundary>:` prompt, type **on** to turn on an existing boundary that you had turned off, **off** to turn off an existing boundary, or **d** to delete an existing boundary. To create a new boundary, press Enter. You then have a choice of creating a polygonal or a rectangular boundary. Press Enter to create a rectangular boundary and pick two corners of the rectangle. Type **p** to create a polygonal boundary and pick all the points you want to create the boundary. Press Enter to complete the boundary. AutoCAD displays only the portion of the xref inside the boundary.

Use the Clipdepth option to create front and back planes for 3D xrefs.

More Stuff

XCLIP also works on blocks.

XLINE

Draws an infinite line (used for construction lines).

 Toolbar: On the Draw toolbar, click the Construction Line button.

Menu: Choose Draw⇨Construction Line.

How to Use It

AutoCAD prompts for a first point. Because this line theoretically is an infinite line, the point really just defines where the line will be. Pick a second through point. AutoCAD creates the xline. Now matter how far out you zoom, the line always goes from one end of your screen to the other.

You also can use horizontal and vertical options. You pick one point, and XLINE creates a horizontal or vertical xline. For the Angle option, you specify an angle — either by typing it or referencing it to a selected object and then typing an angle relative to that object. Then pick a through point.

You can draw an xline that bisects (cuts in half) an angle vertex. Use the Bisect option; then pick an angle vertex, start point, and end point.

The Offset option creates an xline parallel to another object. Type an offset distance, select a line, and pick a point that indicates what side to offset. Alternately, use the Through suboption to specify the offset distance by picking a through point.

More Stuff

See also the RAY command.

XPLODE

Breaks blocks and other compound objects into individual components; gives you control over color, layer, and linetype.

Command line only

How to Use It

XPLODE prompts you to select objects. If you select more than one explodable object, the next prompt asks you whether you want to explode individually or globally. In either case, the suboptions are the same. If you select individual exploding, AutoCAD highlights objects one at a time so that you can make your decisions individually. Following are the options:

Explode	Same as the EXPLODE command.
All	Sets color, linetype, and layer of the individual objects after you explode them. You get the same suboptions as for the Color, LAyer, and Ltype options.
Color	Sets the color of the exploded objects. You can choose any of the standard AutoCAD colors, or you can choose BYBlock or BYLayer. Setting the color to Byblock means that the objects take on the color of the original block.
LAyer	Sets the layer of the exploded objects; otherwise, they take on the current layer.
LType	Sets the linetype of the exploded objects. You can choose BYBlock, BYLayer, CONTinuous, or other loaded linetypes. Setting the linetype to Byblock means that the objects take on the linetype of the original block.
Inherit from parent block	This is what happens to baby blocks when parents die. But in AutoCAD language, it means that the color, linetype, and layer of the exploded objects are the same as the exploded block if its layer is 0 and the linetype is BYBLOCK.

XREF & XATTACH

Manages references to external files. (Xref stands for external references in AutoSpeak.)

 Toolbar: On the Reference toolbar, click the External Reference button.

Menu: Choose Insert⇨External Reference.

How to Use It

Xrefs are external drawings that you insert into your drawing. You use xrefs in much the same way that you use blocks. The main value of xrefs is that each time you open or plot your drawing, the xrefs are reloaded, so any changes in the external drawings are

166 XREF & XATTACH

reflected in your drawing. Also, the actual external drawing is not a part of your drawing — your drawing only contains a reference to the other drawing, keeping drawing size smaller.

The External Reference dialog box is new for Release 14. This dialog box lists your xrefs in a plain list, if the List View button is depressed. If the Tree View button is depressed, your xrefs are listed in hierarchical format so that you can see if any xrefs are nested inside other xrefs.

To attach an xref, click Attach. In the Select file to attach dialog box, choose a file and click Open. The Attach Xref dialog box opens where you can specify the insertion point, scale and rotation, to choose to specify them on-screen. Click OK. The XATTACH command opens the Attach Xref dialog box without any intermediate steps.

In the External Reference dialog box, you can choose any listed xref and use the buttons to do the following:

Detach	Erases the xref and deletes the reference to the external drawing. The advantage of using this option instead of simply erasing the xref is that you also get rid of the layers, colors, linetypes, and other elements of the xref.
Reload	If someone else changes the external drawing while you're working in your drawing, you can reload the xref to see the changes. (Wait until that person has finished making the changes!)
Unload	Removes the xref's display. However, the reference is still available so that you can reload it at any time.
Bind	Turns an xref into a block and cuts the reference to the external drawing. You have two choices: binding, which keeps the xref's layer names in a format that makes where the layer came from clear, and inserting, which strips out the source information.

The bottom of the dialog box displays the location where AutoCAD found the xref. If someone (not you, of course) had the nerve to rename or move the external drawing that you're referencing, your drawing won't be able to find it. Click Browse to find the xref. Click Save Path to save the new name/path.

More Stuff

See the section "Going External" in Chapter 14 of *AutoCAD Release 14 For Dummies*.

'ZOOM

Magnifies or shrinks the display of objects in your drawing.

Toolbar: On the Standard toolbar, use the Zoom flyout.

Menu: Choose View➪Zoom.

How to Use It

Release 14 introduces real-time Zoom which enables you to zoom in and out as you move the cursor. Choose Zoom Realtime from the Standard toolbar. Move the magnifying glass cursor up to zoom in and down to zoom out. Press Esc or Enter to exit real-time zoom mode — or start another command using a menu or toolbar. Right click to open a menu that enables you to switch to pan mode, exit, or use other ZOOM options.

AutoCAD offers lots of zooming options. Each option has a separate icon on the Zoom flyout.

Zoom Previous	Previous	Displays the preceding view. You can use this option up to 10 times before AutoCAD forgets.
Zoom Window	Window	Pick two opposite corners of the display that you want to see.
	Dynamic	This option is a way of panning and zooming at the same time. The display zooms out, and a view box appears. This view box alternates between pan and zoom mode. The box starts out as a pan box, indicated by an X in the middle. Drag the box until you find the location in the drawing that you want; then click that location. You switch to zoom mode, which is indicated by an arrow at one edge. Move your mouse, and you see that the view box changes size instead of moving around the drawing. Resize the box until you have the window that you want to see. Press Enter to complete the command, or click to return to pan mode.
	Scale (X/XP)	Typing a number scales the display relative to the drawing limits. If you type **3**, the display appears three times the size that you'd see after using Zoom with the All option. This option can be confusing if you have another zoom value. So you can type **3x**, which scales the display relative to your current view. If you type **3xp**, AutoCAD scales the display relative to paper space units; use this format when in paper space.

'ZOOM

Center	First, pick a center point for the new view; then specify a magnification or height. A height is a plain number that represents drawing units. Type **10**, for example, to get a display that is 10 drawing units high. To specify magnification, type a number followed by x — for example, **10x**, which magnifies the display by 10.
In	Equivalent to using ZOOM Scale 2x — that is, it doubles the size of the display.
Out	Equivalent to using ZOOM Scale .5x — that is, it halves the size of the display.
All	AutoCAD zooms to the drawing limits or extents, whichever is greater. If you're using a 3D view, this option is equivalent to using ZOOM Extents.
Extents	Displays the entire extents of the drawing.

More Stuff

Another option is Aerial View. (*See also* the DSVIEWER command.)

The System Variables

In this part of the book, you enter the exotic, arcane world of system variables. *System variables* are simply values that AutoCAD stores for all sorts of settings. These variables enable you to fine-tune the way that AutoCAD works. Many system variables just provide information and, to tell you the truth, a lot of them are used only in AutoLISP programs.

In this part . . .

✔ **Fine-tuning the way AutoCAD works**

✔ **Using system variables to get information**

Using System Variables

Once upon a time, you had to use system variables frequently. Nowadays, many variables are handled automatically by the choices that you make in dialog boxes. When you use the DDIM command to create a dimension style, for example, you're working with system variables without knowing it (which is the best way, believe me). I'm including only the system variables that aren't accessible by regular commands, as well as a few other variables that are more convenient to use on the command line. You may want to use these variables directly. I left out some additional system variables that apply only to customizing AutoCAD or using AutoLISP program routines.

I categorized the system variables by type to help you find them more easily.

Simply type the name of the system variable on the command line, followed by its value. You can press Enter after the name of the system variable or just use a space. Press Enter after the value to complete the process. If the system variable just provides information, simply press Enter after you type in the system variable name. Many system variables only turn things on and off. A value of 0 means off; a value of 1 means on — usually!

To see the options available for a system variable, type the system variable name, press Enter, and press F1.

Most lists of system variables are not very useful, but on the rare occasions when you need to use a system variable, look here. I hope this list can speed you on your way. (For more information, choose Help➪AutoCAD Help Topics. From the Contents tab, double-click Command Reference and then System Variables.)

3D

DISPSILH. Related to the ISOLINES system variable, which sets the number of lines on a 3D surface. DISPSILH turns on (1) and off (0) the display of silhouette curves of surface objects in wire-frame mode, so that no matter which viewpoint you use, you always see an isoline showing you the shape of the curve.

FACETRES. Affects the smoothness of 3D objects that are shaded or have hidden lines. You can set this variable from .01 to 10.

HIDEPRECISION. Controls the precision of calculations for hides and shades. The default, 0, uses normal precision. Set it to 1 to specify double precision to calculate the hide. A setting of 1 requires more memory than a setting of 0.

ISOLINES. The number of isolines per surface on an object; they can range from 0 to 2047. The default is 4, which is pretty puny.

SHADEDGE. Controls the way edges are shaded. Values are

0	Shades faces, but edges not highlighted
1	Shades faces and highlights edges
2	Doesn't shade faces, hides hidden lines, shows edges
3	Highlights edges only, with no lighting effect

Even though 1 probably is the most useful setting, 3 is the default.

SHADEDIF. Sets the percent of diffuse reflective light to ambient light. The default is 70. You may find 50 to be a useful value. Values can range from 0 to 100.

SURFTAB1. The number of tabulations used in the RULESURF and TABSURF commands. Also, for the REVSURF and EDGESURF commands, this variable sets the M (row) direction.

SURFTAB2. Sets the N (column) direction for the REVSURF and EDGESURF commands.

SURFU. The surface density in the M (row) direction. Applies to polyface meshes, such as the meshes created by 3DMESH.

SURFV. The surface density in the N (column) direction. Applies to polyface meshes, such as the meshes created by 3DMESH.

UCSFOLLOW. Determines whether AutoCAD returns you to plan view when you change the UCS. A value of 0 means that you don't return to plan view; 1 means that you do. The default is 0.

Attributes

ATTDIA. Determines whether you get a dialog box when you use the INSERT command to insert a block that contains attributes. A setting of 0 says that you don't get the dialog box; a setting of 1 says that you do.

ATTREQ. If you set to 0, AutoCAD uses default attribute values when you insert a block with attributes. If you set to 1, AutoCAD prompts you for values. The default is 1.

Dimensioning

DIMASO. Turns associative dimensioning on and off. If associative dimensioning is off, the parts of the dimension are separate objects and don't adjust when you change the dimensioned objects. The variable's values are ON and OFF.

DIMSHO. When this variable is on, associative dimensions are recomputed continually as you drag an object. (Associative dimensions change automatically when you change the object.) If this feature slows your computer, turn DIMSHO off.

DIMSOXD. Suppresses dimension lines that otherwise would be outside extension lines. (DIMSOXD is not a baseball team.)

Drawing Aids

BLIPMODE. Turns blips on and off.

EXPERT. This variable is for the experts among you who get annoyed when AutoCAD asks things such as `Block already defined. Redefine it?` ("Of course, I want to redefine it; why do you think I'm doing this?") A value of 0 is the normal setting. Values ranging from 1 to 5 suppress more and more prompts.

MAXACTVP. Specifies the maximum number of viewports that are regenerated at one time. The default is 16.

MEASUREINIT. Sets the type of measurement used, English using the ANSI standard (setting of 0) or Metric using ISO standards (setting of 1) when you open an existing drawing. This setting affects which hatch pattern and linetype file AutoCAD uses. The default varies according to your country.

PICKSTYLE. Determines the way groups and hatches can be selected.

0	No group selection. Hatches are selected without their boundaries.
1	Group selection. Hatches are selected without their boundaries.
2	No group selection. Hatches are selected along with their boundaries.
3	Group selection. Hatches are selected along with their boundaries.

RTDISPLAY. Controls how AutoCAD displays raster images during realtime zoom or pan. Set this system variable to 0 to display the raster image (this setting can slow down your panning and zooming). Set it to 1 (the default) to display an outline only.

VISRETAIN. Sets the visibility of layers in Xref files. A setting of 0 means that Xrefs take on the layer definition in the current drawing. A setting of 1 means that the layer settings in the Xref drawing take precedence.

WORLDVIEW. Determines whether the UCS changes to the WCS when you use DVIEW or VPOINT. A value of 0 means that the UCS remains unchanged; a value of 1 means that it switches to the WCS.

Edits

DELOBJ. Determines whether objects used to create other objects are maintained in the drawing database. The default (1) retains these objects; a value of 0 deletes them.

EXPLMODE. Determines whether EXPLODE explodes blocks that are nonuniformly scaled (NUS), which means that the X and Y scales are different. The default is to explode them (value of 1), but you can turn the feature off (0).

MIRRTEXT. When you're mirroring objects that include text, a value of 1 (the default) mirrors the text just like anything else. A value of 0 keeps the text looking normal, so that you don't need to look into a mirror to read it. This variable is a good one to know.

Information/Customization

Most of these variables provide information only. Many of the variables are *read-only*, which means that you can look at them and sigh, but you can't change anything.

ACADPREFIX. The directory path of the ACAD environment.

ACADVER. The AutoCAD version number.

AUDITCTL. Determines the creation of an audit report file.

CDATE. Sets the date and time.

CMDACTIVE. Stores what kind of command is active.

CMDDIA. Turns dialog boxes on and off. If you set this variable to 0, you won't see dialog boxes. The default is 1.

CMDNAMES. The name of the active command.

DATE. The date and time in Julian format.

DBMOD. The drawing modification status.

DCTCUST. The custom spelling dictionary file.

DCTMAIN. The main spelling dictionary file.

DISTANCE. The distance calculated by the DIST command.

DWGNAME. The drawing name.

DWGPREFIX. The directory path for the drawing.

DWGTITLED. Indicates whether you've named your drawing.

EXTMAX. The upper-right corner of the drawing extents.

EXTMIN. The lower-left corner of the drawing extents.

FILEDIA. Turns on and off the display of dialog boxes that deal with files, such as the Open dialog box.

FILENAME. Stores the filename.

LASTANGLE. The end angle of the last arc that you drew.

LASTPOINT. The last point entered.

LASTPROMPT. Stores the last text string that appears on the command line, including user input.

LIMMAX. The upper-right drawing limits.

LIMMIN. The lower-left drawing limits.

LOCALE. The ISO (International Standards Organization) language code of the current AutoCAD version.

LOGINNAME. The user's name (probably you). This is for networks that require a login name.

MENUECHO. Sets menu echo and display prompting.

MENUNAME. The current menu name.

PERIMETER. The last perimeter value calculated by AREA, LIST, or DBLIST.

PFACEVMAX. The maximum number of vertices per face.

PLATFORM. The computer platform that you're using (Windows 95, Windows NT 3.51, or Windows NT 4.0., stage right, stage left, and so on).

PLOTID. Changes the default printer, based on the description you assigned when you configured AutoCAD.

PLOTTER. Changes the default printer, based on its assigned number, starting from 0.

RASTERPREVIEW. Determines whether drawing preview images are saved with the drawing and what type of images are saved.

SAVEFILE. Stores the filename that AutoCAD uses in auto-saving. Set the auto-save time by choosing Tools➪Preferences➪System tab.

SAVENAME. Stores the filename to which you save the drawing.

SCREENSIZE. The size, in pixels, of the current viewport.

SHPNAME. The default shape name.

TDCREATE. The date and time the drawing was created.

TEMPPREFIX. Sets a directory name for temporary files.

TREEDEPTH. Configures the spatial index, which structures the database of objects.

TREEMAX. Limits the size of the spatial index, saving memory.

VIEWCTR. The center of the view of the current viewport.

VSMAX. The upper-right corner of the virtual screen.

VSMIN. The lower-left corner of the virtual screen.

WORLDUCS. Stores whether the UCS is the same as the World Coordinate System. A value of 0 means that the UCS is different; a value of 1 means that the UCS and the WCS are the same.

Object Creation

INSNAME. Stores a default block name for DDINSERT or INSERT.

PELLIPSE. Determines whether the ELLIPSE command creates a true ellipse or a polyline representation of one. A value of 0 (the default) draws a true ellipse. A value of 1 creates a polyline representation of an ellipse. This concept of a polyline ellipse is a holdover from previous releases of AutoCAD.

PLINEGEN. When set the 0, the default, linetypes start each vertex of a polyline with a dash. When set to 1, the linetype is generated in a continuous pattern regardless of the vertices.

PLINETYPE. The value controls the conversion and creation of Release 14 lightweight polylines. At 0, polylines in previous release drawings aren't converted when opened in Release 14, and AutoCAD creates the old-format polylines. At 1, polylines in previous release drawings aren't converted when opened in Release 14, and AutoCAD creates lightweight polylines. At 2 (the default), polylines in previous release drawings are converted when opened in Release 14, and AutoCAD creates lightweight polylines. This system variable affects all commands that create polylines, for example PLINE, RECTANG, POLYGON, and so on.

POLYSIDES. The default number of sides for polygon.

SKPOLY. A value of 0 means that SKETCH creates lines; a value of 1 means that it creates polylines.

SPLFRAME. Sets spline-fit polyline display. If the value is 0, the frame that controls a spline or polygon mesh isn't displayed; also, invisible edges of 3D faces and polyface meshes aren't displayed. If the value is 1, you see the frame of a spline or polygon mesh and invisible edges of 3D faces and polyface meshes.

SPLINESEGS. Sets the number of line segments that each spline generates. A higher number results in a curve that more precisely matches the frame.

SPLINETYPE. Determines type of spline curve created by PEDIT spline. Choose 5 for quadratic B-spline; 6 for cubic B-spline.

SURFTYPE. Sets the type of surface fitting used by the PEDIT Smooth option for 3D Polygon Meshes. Type **5** for a quadratic B-spline, **6** for a cubic B-spline, and **8** for a Bezier surface.

Text

FONTALT. Sets an alternative font that AutoCAD uses, if the font that you ask for can't be found. (Little AutoCAD lost her fonts and didn't know where to find them.)

TEXTQLTY. Sets the resolution of TrueType 1 fonts. Values represent dots per inch. Now only affects rendering, printer or plotter output, and exporting with PSOUT.

TEXTSIZE. Stores the default or last height for text styles without a fixed height.

TEXTSTYLE. The current text-style name.

Part IV

The Menus and Toolbars

This part guides you through the menus and toolbars. If you want to do something in AutoCAD but don't know the command name, try looking here. Menus and toolbars are usually organized by function; you can skim through the possibilities and find the command you need.

In this part . . .

- Finding commands on menus and submenus
- Finding buttons on toolbars and flyouts

Using Menus and Toolbars

The menu items and toolbar ToolTips are not always the same as the command name. Although they usually make more sense, the command names are often in unintelligible abbreviations. Luckily, when you choose a menu item or toolbar button, the command name appears on the command line (well, most of the time).

Here's how you find the name of the command:

1. Choose a menu item or toolbar button that looks useful.

2. At the next prompt, press Esc to cancel the command.

3. Look on the command line. You should see the name of the command. If the command name scrolls by too fast for you to see, press F2 to open the text screen. (Press F2 again to return to your drawing.)

4. Look up the command in Part II of this book.

Here's a warning about the ToolTips that are supposed to give you some tip about the function of the button. Sometimes a tip such as the one AutoCAD gives you can be your worst enemy. The most you can say is that it's sometimes like a foul tip when the batter has two strikes: It keeps you in the game but doesn't get you much of anywhere. And those little pictures are not always very communicative of the button's function either — sometimes, a word is worth a thousand pictures. This part includes the ToolTip name next to each button, and occasionally an explanatory footnote when the ToolTip seems to do more harm than good. Also, don't forget to look on the status bar when the ToolTip pops up for the short explanation that appears — it may provide the information you need.

Some of the toolbars have flyouts. You can tell which ones they are by the little black arrow at the bottom of the button. The flyouts are also available as toolbars. For the buttons that have flyouts, I indicate the flyout name. You can then find the buttons listed under the toolbar of the same name. For example, the Standard toolbar contains a button called Named Views. This is just the first button on the Viewpoint flyout. Look up the Viewpoint toolbar to see all the buttons. (By the way, by default, if you click another button on a flyout — not the top one — the one you clicked moves to the top.)

AutoCAD Menus

The File menu

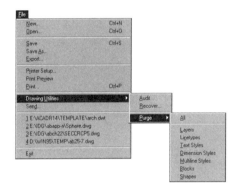

Choosing File⇨Print is equivalent to using the PLOT command.

The Edit menu

Edit⇨Cut, Edit⇨Copy, and Edit⇨Paste are equivalent to the CUTCLIP, COPYCLIP, and PASTECLIP commands.

The View menu

View⇨Tiled Viewports is grayed out (unavailable) if the TILE button on the status bar is grayed out (off).

View⇨Floating Viewports is grayed out (unavailable) if the TILE button on the status bar is darkened (on).

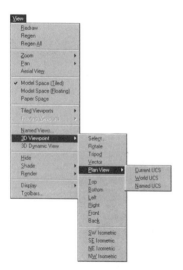

AutoCAD Menus

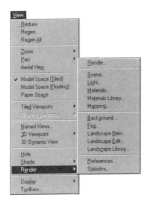

The Insert menu

182 AutoCAD Menus

The Format menu

The Tools menu

AutoCAD Menus

The Draw menu

AutoCAD Menus

AutoCAD Menus

The Dimension menu

The Modify menu

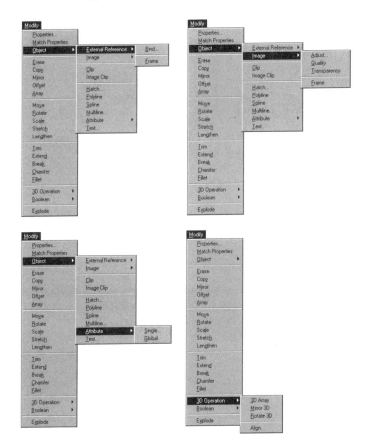

186 AutoCAD Toolbars

The Help menu

AutoCAD Toolbars

The Standard toolbar

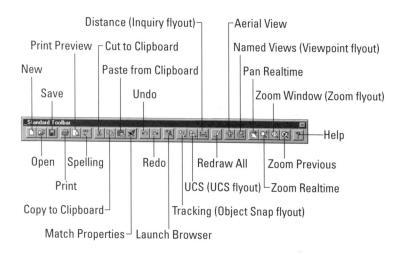

AutoCAD Toolbars

+ Clicking Save executes the QSAVE command.
+ As mentioned under the Edit menu, Print is really the PLOT command.
+ Cut to Clipboard, Copy to Clipboard, and Paste from Clipboard are the CUTCLIP, COPYCLIP, and PASTECLIP commands, respectively.

The Object Snap flyout/toolbar

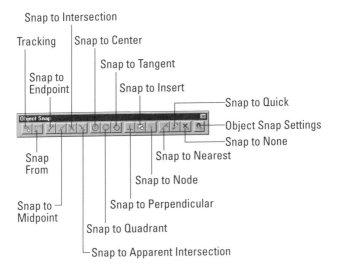

The UCS flyout/toolbar

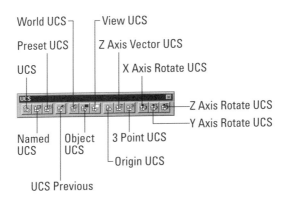

188 AutoCAD Toolbars

The Inquiry flyout/toolbar

Distance
 Mass Properties

 Area   Locate Point
    List

Clicking Locate Point executes the ID command.

The Viewpoint flyout/toolbar

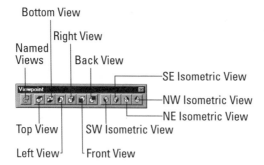

Bottom View
 Right View
Named
Views   Back View
           SE Isometric View
           NW Isometric View
           NE Isometric View
Top View   SW Isometric View
Left View   Front View

The Zoom flyout/toolbar

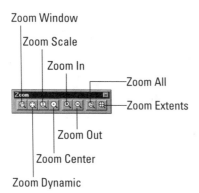

Zoom Window
 Zoom Scale
  Zoom In
          Zoom All
          Zoom Extents
   Zoom Out
  Zoom Center
Zoom Dynamic

AutoCAD Toolbars 189

The Object Properties toolbar

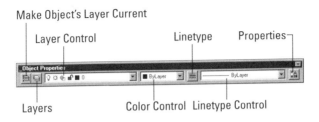

- **See also** Part I for an explanation of how to use Make Object's Layer Current.

- Use Layers to create layers. Use Layer Control to set the current layer and to change the state (On/Off, Thawed/Frozen, Unlocked/Locked) of a layer.

- Properties is equivalent to the DDMODIFY command if you choose one object and equivalent to DDCHPROP if you choose more than one object.

The Draw toolbar

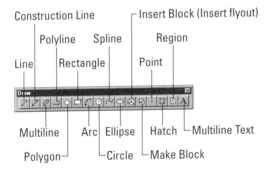

Construction line is the same as an xline. *See also* the XLINE command.

190 AutoCAD Toolbars

The Insert flyout/toolbar

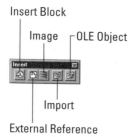

The Modify toolbar

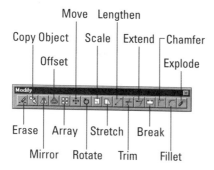

The External Reference toolbar

The Dimension toolbar

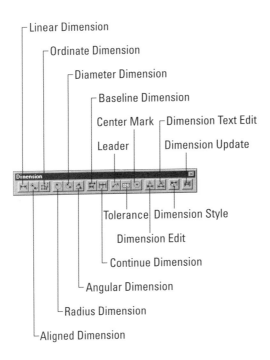

The Modify II toolbar

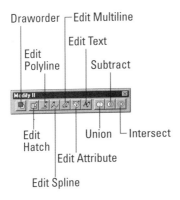

192 AutoCAD Toolbars

The Reference toolbar

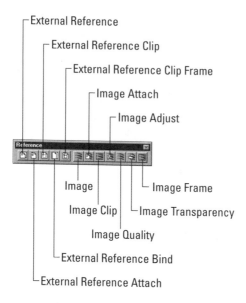

The Render toolbar

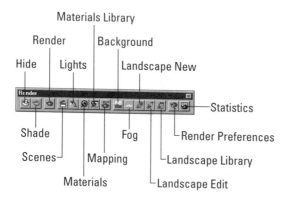

AutoCAD Toolbars

The Solids toolbar

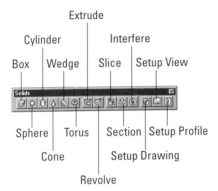

The Surfaces toolbar

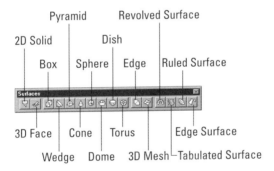

The Internet Utilities toolbar

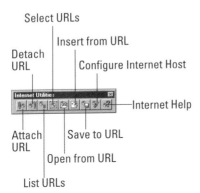

AutoCAD Toolbars

NOTE

To display this toolbar, the `inet` menu group must be loaded. Choose Tools⇨Customize Menus to load it. If this menu group isn't listed, choose Browse to locate it. Then right-click any toolbar to open the Toolbars dialog box. In the Menu Group drop-down list at the bottom of the dialog box, choose inet. Then choose Internet Utilities from the Toolbars list and close the Toolbars dialog box. No menu exists for Internet Utilities, just a toolbar.

Techie Talk

The terms used in AutoCAD often are so obscure that understanding how to use the program becomes difficult, a concept I call AutoSpeak in this book (after Newspeak in George Orwell's *1984*). I hope that this glossary helps you; it includes some of the terms that always stumped me.

ACAD environment variable. Tells AutoCAD the drive and folder of certain files that it needs.

ActiveX Automation. Enables the AutoCAD user to use programming languages such as Visual Basic to program AutoCAD. These programs can integrate AutoCAD with applications such as Excel and Word.

ADI. *AutoCAD Device Interface.* A specification created by Autodesk, the creator of AutoCAD, that sets standards for drivers, printers, screens, plotters, and so on.

alias. A short name for an AutoCAD command. You can customize the ACAD.PGP file to create your own — for example, CI for CIRCLE and CO for COPY.

ambient light. Overall background light used for rendering. *See also* the RENDER and LIGHT commands.

annotation. Text, dimensions, tolerances, symbols, or notes that explain a drawing.

aperture. The little box that appears when you use an object snap. The aperture is different from the pickbox.

Techie Talk

aspect ratio. The ratio of width to height on a computer screen. The aspect ratio is used for importing and exporting graphics. You also have an Aspect option for the SNAP and GRID commands that enables you to use different X and Y spacings.

associative. Applies to dimensions and hatches; means that these elements adjust themselves when you change the objects to which they're attached.

attribute. Text attached to a block that can be assigned a specific value each time that the block is inserted. All these values can be extracted and turned into a database, such as a bill of materials. *See also* the DDATTDEF and ATTEXT commands.

AutoLISP. The AutoCAD version of the LISP programming language. You can use AutoLISP to write programs that control the way that AutoCAD functions.

AutoSnap. AutoCAD's way of letting you know when you're in the neighborhood of an object snap. You see a Snap Tip with the object snap's type (Endpoint, Midpoint, or such) as well as a marker — a shape that indicates the object snap's location. You also feel a slight pull of the cursor toward the object snap.

B-spline. A curve defined by points that you choose; also called a *NURBS curve*. *See also* the SPLINE and SPLINEDIT commands. *See also* the SPLINETYPE and SURFTYPE system variables.

Bezier curve. A type of B-spline curve. *See also* SURFTYPE.

bind. To turn an external reference (xref) into a regular block.

bitmap. A type of graphic defined by pixel or dots (rather than by vectors).

blips. Little markers on the screen that show where you specified a point. REDRAW gets rid of blips. *See also* BLIPMODE.

block. One or more objects grouped to create a single object.

Boolean operation. Adding, subtracting, or intersecting solids or 2D regions.

boundary. A closed region or polyline. *See also* BOUNDARY.

BYLAYER. Means that an object takes its color and linetype from its layer definition; you don't set the color and linetype.

Cartesian coordinate system. A way of defining point locations using three perpendicular X,Y,Z axes.

chord. A line that connects two points on a circle or arc. *See also* the ARC command.

clipping planes. Planes that cut off the field of view. *See also* DVIEW.

color map. A table that defines color in terms of red, green, and blue (RGB) intensity. Anytime you use the color slider bars or color wheel, you're using the color map. *See also* DDCOLOR.

control point. A point (usually, many points) that AutoCAD creates to define a spline. *See also* fit points.

cycling. A way of going through all the object snap points within the aperture box. Press Tab until you get the object snap you want.

digitizer. An electronic flat board that enables you to draw and execute commands with the tablet template. You use something called a puck or stylus, which is similar to a mouse but has crosshairs that provide for exact point specification.

DWF. *Drawing Web File;* a format for a file that can be placed on a Web site. The viewer of the file can pan, zoom, and print, but can't access the actual drawing objects.

DXF. *Drawing Interchange Format;* an ASCII file format that contains all the

Techie Talk

information of a drawing. DXF is used to import or export drawings between programs.

entity. Another word for an object (anything in your drawing).

environment. The location of and settings for other files on which AutoCAD depends, such as acad.dwt (the default template).

explode. To break a block into its original objects. *See also* the EXPLODE and XPLODE commands.

external reference (xref). Another file that's referenced in your file, creating a link between the two. *See also* the XREF command.

fence. A set of lines that you use to select objects. Anything that crosses the fence gets sent to jail for trespassing. *See also* the SELECT command.

fit points. Points that you specify when defining a spline. *See also* control points.

floating viewports. Bordered views of a drawing that show different viewpoints and/or zooms of your objects. Floating viewports, which are created in paper space with tilemode off, are objects that you can move, resize, and delete.

flyout. A bunch of hidden buttons that fly out when you click the top button. A flyout is equivalent to a secondary menu.

freeze. A mode for a layer that means that the layer isn't displayed, regenerated, or plotted.

grid. A rectangular grid of regularly spaced dots that cover the screen. Grids help you get a feel for the unit size and assist you in drawing; if you don't like them, just grid and bear it. Otherwise, *see also* the GRID and DDRMODES commands.

grips. Small squares that appear on objects when you select them. You can use grips to modify the objects directly. *See also* DDGRIPS.

group. A named group of objects that you can select and modify as a group. *See also* the GROUP command.

hatch. A pattern of lines (or a solid fill) used to fill a closed area to indicate shading or a type of material (bricks, grass, and so on).

hidden surfaces. Surfaces that would be hidden from a certain viewpoint. These surfaces are hidden when using HIDE, SHADE, or RENDER.

island. An enclosed area within a hatch area — for example, a small circle within a big circle. *See also* the BHATCH command.

isolines. Lines that AutoCAD uses to show the curve of a surface. Isolines are similar to tessellation lines.

isometric drawing. A drawing that places the X,Y,Z axes 120 degrees from one another and is used in 2D drawing to give the appearance of 3D objects.

lightweight polyline. A new type of polyline for Release 14 that requires less memory to store. It replaces the old type of polyline, but you draw polylines in the same way as in Release 13.

linetype. A type of line. Linetype indicates whether the line is continuous or formed of dots, dashes, and spaces.

M direction. When AutoCAD draws 3D meshes, the M direction is set by the way that you define the first and second rows. But because you're in 3D, a row can face in any direction.

M size. When AutoCAD draws polygon meshes, the M size is the number of rows.

mass properties. Properties of an object that has volume, such as center of gravity.

materials. Materials are used in rendering. Materials are called by the names of real materials — such as steel, glass, and plastic — and are defined by their color, reflective qualities, roughness (which affects highlights created by a light source), transparency and so on. Materials are attached to objects. *See also* the RMAT, MATLIB, and RENDER commands.

mesh (or mesh surface). A bunch of connected polygons that create faces and that together represent the surface of a curved object. By specifying the vertices of the polygons, you define the surface. A mesh has no mass or weight properties (unlike solids) but can be shaded and rendered. *See also* the 3D, 3DMESH, PFACE, RULESURF, TABSURF, REVSURF, and EDGESURF commands.

model. A 2D or 3D drawing of a real object. AutoCAD has three 3D model types: wire frame, surface, and solid.

model space. The place where you create models, which means where you draw. Model space is different from paper space, in which you can lay out your drawing for plotting (if you want). *See also* the MSPACE command.

node. The same as a point. You use the Node object snap to locate a point object.

normal. A line that is perpendicular to a plane or surface; used to define a new plane in some editing commands. *See also* the SLICE and SECTION commands.

Noun/Verb Selection. Selecting the object (noun) before the command (verb). *See also* the DDSELECT command.

NURBS. Stands for *nonuniform rational B-spline;* a B-spline defined by a series of points.

object. Anything that's considered to be one element in your drawing, such as a line, a circle, or a line of text. An object is the same as an entity.

object snap. Called OSNAP in AutoSpeak; geometric points on an object that you can select automatically — for example, endpoints, midpoints, and circle centers.

ortho mode. A setting that limits you to drawing horizontally or vertically.

orthogonal. Having perpendicular intersections.

paper space. A drawing mode used for laying out a drawing for plotting. In paper space, you create floating viewports with different views of your drawing. *See also* the PSPACE, MVSETUP, and MVIEW commands.

parallel projection. A way of viewing a 3D object without showing perspective. *See also* the DVIEW command.

pickbox. The little box that appears at the cursor when you see a `Select objects` prompt. You can change the size of the pickbox by using the DDSELECT command.

pixel. Short for picture element. Pixels are the teensy-weensy dots that make up the picture on your screen. Certain graphics programs enable you to change graphics pixel by pixel.

plan view. The view of an object looking straight down from above. Plan view is the only accurate view for 2D objects but only one possible view for 3D objects.

point filters. A way of extracting a coordinate point by filtering out one or two of the X, Y, or Z coordinates. *See also* the section on filters in Part I.

polyline. A group of lines and arcs that are treated as one object. *See also* the PLINE and PEDIT commands.

primitive. A basic 3D shape, such as a box, wedge, cone, cylinder, sphere, or torus.

puck. A tool for drawing and choosing menu or toolbar commands when you have a digitizer. It looks somewhat like a mouse but has a transparent area with crosshairs for precise picking of points.

raster image. An image or graphics created by converting math or digital information into a series of dots.

realtime pan and zoom. A way of panning and zooming in which the display changes as you move the mouse cursor.

redraw. To refresh the screen, thereby getting rid of blip marks and stray remains of editing commands.

reflection. The levels of highlights created by light on a surface. *See also* the RMAT command.

region. A closed 2D area. *See also* the REGION command.

right-hand rule. A hokey but effective way to figure out which way is up (which way the Z axis goes). Hold the back of your right hand near the screen. Point your thumb in the direction of the positive X axis. Point your index finger up in the direction of the positive Y axis. Stick your other fingers straight out at right angles to your index finger. That's the direction of the positive Z axis.

roughness. The spread of the highlight produced by a material's reflection. *See also* the RMAT command.

ruled surface. A surface created between two curves or between a point and a curve. *See also* the RULESURF command.

running object snap. An object snap that stays on until you turn it off. If you have a running endpoint object snap, every time you select an object, you're selecting the endpoint of the object. It's also a warning that if you run into an object, something might go snap. *See also* the DDOSNAP command.

selection set. The group of objects that you've selected.

shape. A special kind of object that's been defined with certain customization codes and compiled into a compressed form. *Shape* usually refers to fonts; it doesn't mean any old regular shape that you draw on your screen.

snap. When snap is on, the cursor jumps to the nearest point defined by the snap spacing; you can't get to anything in between. *See also* the SNAP command.

spline. A smooth curve passing through or near points that you specify. AutoCAD uses a particular kind of spline called a NURBS (nonuniform rational B-spline) curve. (Sounds nurby to me.)

stylus. A tool for drawing and choosing items from a menu or toolbar when you have a digitizer. It looks somewhat like a pen and is appropriate for drawing where you need fine control.

support file search path. Where AutoCAD looks for supporting files containing fonts, drawings to insert, menus, linetypes, and hatch patterns. You can add any folder on your hard drive to the support file search path using the Files tab of the Preferences dialog box (*see also* the PREFERENCES command).

surface. A topological 2D area. You can create a surface by using surface commands, such as 3D, 3DMESH, TABSURF, RULESURF, and REVSURF.

system variable. Variables storing modes and values that affect the way that AutoCAD functions. Some system variables are read-only; many others, you can set. *See also* Part III for an exhaustive (and exhausting) list.

Techie Talk

tabulated surface. A kind of ruled surface defined by a curve and a line or polyline that indicates a direction.

template. A file that contains certain settings (layers, styles, and so on) and is used as the basis for new drawings.

temporary files. AutoCAD creates temporary files during a drawing session. These files usually are closed when you exit, but if your system crashes, they may be left on your hard disk.

tessellation lines. Lines that help you visualize a curved, 3D surface.

tiled model space. A drawing mode in which you can divide the drawing space into viewports that can't be overlapped and that are arranged next to one another like floor tiles. *See also* the TILEMODE system variable as well as the VPORTS command, which creates multiple tiled viewports.

tolerances. The amount of variance allowable in an object, shown after a dimension. Tolerances can be shown as limits tolerances or plus/minus tolerances.

ToolTip. The description of a button when you put the cursor over a toolbar button for a couple of seconds. ToolTips are supposed to be helpful.

Tracking. A substitute for point filters that enables you to locate a point based on the coordinates of existing objects.

transparent commands. Commands that can be used while you're in the middle of another command. Transparent commands appear with an apostrophe in front of the command name, because that's how you type them in the command line.

unit. Any distance that you use for measuring purposes. The unit is the basis of all coordinates. When you plot your drawing, you can set the unit equal to inches or millimeters. *See also* UNITS.

User Coordinate System. A coordinate system that you define by specifying where (relative to the World Coordinate System) the origin is, as well as the direction of the X,Y,Z axes. *See also* UCS.

vector. Any object that has direction and length, such as a line.

viewpoint. A location in 3D from which you can view your drawing.

viewport. A rectangular box that contains all or part of your drawing. Two kinds of viewports exist: tiled and floating. Tiled viewports are used in model space with the TILEMODE system variable on. Floating viewports are used in paper space with the TILEMODE system variable off; these viewports are actual objects that you can edit. *See also* the TILEMODE system variable; *see also* the VPORTS, MVIEW, MSPACE, and PSPACE commands.

virtual screen. An imaginary screen held in memory that enables AutoCAD to quickly translate complex coordinates held in the database into actual coordinates on your screen.

WHIP! plug-in or ActiveX control. A program that enables you to view DWF files. Use the plug-in, if you use the Netscape browser and use the ActiveX control if you use the Internet Explorer browser. WHIP! is available free of charge at Autodesk's Web site.

wire frame. A representation of a 3D object made using lines and arcs. Also, the display of surfaces and solids that looks like it's made out of lines and arcs.

World Coordinate System. A coordinate system that is used as the basis for all other systems that you may define.

Index

Symbols & Numbers

* (asterisk), 162
<> (angle brackets), 9
= (equal sign), 162
' (apostrophe), 9
/ (slash), 9
. (period), 18
... (ellipsis), 10
? (question mark), 22
3D command, 26–27
3DARRAY command, 27
3DFACE command, 28
3DPOLY command, 28–29

A

ACADPREFIX system variable, 173
ACADVER system variable, 173
ACI (AutoCAD Color Index), 130
ActiveX Automation, 23
Aerial View, 20, 67
ALIGN command, 29
aligning
  blocks, 65
  dimensions, 58
  objects, with other objects, 29
  text, 68
  viewports, 107
ambient light, 90, 129, 171
angles
  dimension text, 58
  display, 55–56
  right, 19, 20
  rotation, of text, 32
  smoothing, 126
  taper, 76
  units of measurement, 12, 55–56
  xline, 164
annotation, 88–89
aperture, 29, 196
'APERTURE command, 29
ARC command, 30
arcs
  angle, changing, 89–90
  angle measurement, 59
  center mark, drawing, 60
  center point, 114
  diameter dimension for, 61
  direction of, 114
  drawing, 30
  extending, 75–76, 90–91
  in polylines, 114–115
  radial dimension for, 63–64
  resolution, 158
  revolving, 128
area
  calculating, 30
  overlapping, 84–85, 86
  for regions, 97, 147
AREA command, 30
ARRAY command, 30–31
associative dimensioning, 171–172
ATTACHURL command, 31
ATTDIA system variable, 45, 171
ATTDISP command, 31–32
ATTEDIT command, 32
ATTREDEF command, 33
ATTREQ system variable, 171
attributes
  defined, 31
  defining, 44–45
  editing, 32, 45, 49
  extracting, 46–47
  material, 129–130
  redefining blocks with, 33
  system variables, 171
  text attached, 44
  visibility setting, 31–32
AUDIT command, 33
audit report file, 173
AUDITCTL system variable, 173
AutoSnap, 17, 111
axes, 131–132, 155

B

'BASE command, 33–34
BHATCH command, 34–35
'BLIPMODE command, 35
BLIPMODE system variable, 172
blips, 35, 172
blocks
  aligning, 65
  color setting, 49
  creating, 36
  drawing at intervals, 98–99
  exploding, 51, 75, 164–165, 173
  inserting, 36, 51, 99

(continued)

blocks *(continued)*
  list of, 36
  naming, 36, 65
  redefining, 33
  saving as file, 162
  unused, removing, 120
BMAKE command, 36
boundaries
  creating, 36–37, 93, 163
  deleting, 163
  turning off, 163
BOUNDARY command, 36–37
BOX command, 37–38
BREAK command, 38
BROWSER command, 38–39
BYBLOCK command, 49
BYLAYER command, 49

C

'CAL command, 39
Cartesian coordinates, 14, 15
CDATE system variable, 173
CHAMFER command, 39–40
CHANGE command, 40–41
CIRCLE command, 41
circles
  3D, drawing, 27
  as base of cylinder, 43
  center marks through, 60
  defining, 41
  diameter dimension for, 61
  dimensioning, 59
  drawing, 41
  radial dimensions for, 63–64
  resolution, 158
  revolving, 128
CMDACTIVE system variable, 173
CMDDIA system variable, 173
CMDNAMES system variable, 173
colors
  ambient light, 90, 129
  default, 49
  diffuse, 129
  grip, 50
  layers and, 49
  light, 92
  point, 91
  selecting, 48–49
command line, 9–10
commands. *See also individual commands*
  default, 9
  finding name of, 178
  transparent, 9–10, 201
  undoing, 156–157
compass-and-axis tripod, 57
CONE command, 42

context-sensitive Help, 22
control points, 143
coordinates, 14–19, 55–56, 81
COPY command, 42–43
corners, rounding, 77–78
crosshairs, 8, 119
cursors
  crosshair, 8, 119
  horizontal/vertical restriction of, 110
  snapping to grid, 140
CYLINDER command, 43

D

databases
  attribute data used as, 46–47
  information, listing, 95
  reindexing, 14
  removing data from, 120
DATE system variable, 173
date/time, 149–150, 173, 175
DBLIST command, 43
DBMOD system variable, 173
DCTCUST system variable, 173
DCTMAIN system variable, 173
DDATTDEF command, 44–45
DDATTE command, 45
DDATTEXT command, 46–47
DDCHPROP command, 48
DDCOLOR command, 48–49, 103
DDEDIT command, 45, 49
'DDGRIPS command, 21, 49–50
DDIM command, 11, 13, 50–51, 170
DDINSERT command, 36, 51
DDMODIFY command, 41, 52
'DDPTYPE command, 52
DDRENAME command, 52–53
'DDRMODES command, 53
'DDSELECT command, 20–21, 53–54
DDUCS command, 54–55
DDUCSP command, 55
'DDUNITS command, 12, 55–56
DDVIEW command, 56
DDVPOINT command, 55, 57–58
DELOBJ system variable, 173
dialog boxes, 11, 22, 173, 174
diameter dimensions, 61
digitizing tablet
  calibrating, 147–148
  configuring, 119, 147
  input/output port, reconfiguring, 125
  turning on/off, 148
DIMALIGNED command, 58
DIMANGULAR command, 59
DIMASO system variable, 171
DIMBASELINE command, 60
DIMCENTER command, 60

Index

DIMCONTINUE command, 61
DIMDIAMETER command, 61–62
DIMEDIT command, 62
dimensions
  aligned, 58
  angular, 59, 60, 61
  arc, 59
  circle, 59
  continuing, 61
  diameter, 61
  editing, 62
  linear, 60, 61, 62–63
  ordinate, 60, 61
  radial, 63–64
  styles, 13, 50–51, 120
  text, 62, 64
DIMLINEAR command, 62–63
DIMRADIUS command, 63–64
DIMSHO system variable, 172
DIMSOXD system variable, 172
DIMTEDIT command, 64
DISPSILH system variable, 170
'DIST command, 64–65
distance<angle coordinate display, 15
DISTANCE system variable, 173
distant light, 92
DIVIDE command, 65
DONUT command, 65
donuts
  3D, 27, 152
  drawing, 65
DOS, upgrading from, 3
dragging objects, 66
'DRAGMODE command, 66
Drawing Interchange Format (DXF) files
  creating, 72
  importing, 71–72
drawing limits, 174
Drawing Web Format (DWF) files
  creating, 70–71
  viewing, 71
drawings
  creating, 108
  damaged, repairing, 122
  directory path, 174
  inserting, 51
  name of, 7
  opening, 6–7, 109–110
  printing/plotting, 115–117
  redisplaying, 123–124
  reducing size of, 120
  regenerating, 124
  saving, 8, 120, 133
  setting up, 12
  translating, 75
DRAWORDER command, 66–67
DSVIEWER command, 67–68

DTEXT command, 13, 45, 68
DVIEW command, 69–70, 81
DWFOUT command, 70–71
DWGNAME system variable, 173
DWGPREFIX system variable, 174
DWGTITLED system variable, 174
DXFIN command, 71–72
DXFOUT command, 72
dynamic coordinate display, 15

E

EDGE command, 28, 72–73
edges
  3D Face, visibility of, 72
  filleting, 77–78
  invisible, displaying, 176
  shading, 171
  trimming, 153
EDGESURF command, 73, 171
'ELEV command, 73
ELLIPSE command, 42, 74, 175
ERASE command, 74
EXPERT system variable, 172
EXPLMODE system variable, 173
EXPLODE command, 51, 75
exploding blocks, 51, 75, 164–165, 173
EXPORT command, 75
exporting, 75, 98
EXTEND command, 75–76
external references, 163–166, 172
EXTMAX system variable, 174
EXTMIN system variable, 174
EXTRUDE command, 38, 76

F

FACETRES system variable, 170
FATAL ERROR message, 122
feature control frames, 150
FILEDIA system variable, 174
FILENAME system variable, 174
files
  audit report, 173
  comma-delimited, 47
  DWF, creating, 70–71
  DXF, creating, 72
  extracting attribute data to, 46–47
  log, 96
  saving blocks as, 162
  space-delimited, 47
  temporary, 175
'FILL command, 77
FILLET command, 77–78
'FILTER command, 78–79
filters, 18, 78–79
fit points, 143, 144

floating viewports
  freezing/thawing layers within, 158–160
  managing, 106–107
  specifications for, 107–108
flyouts
  defined, 8, 25
  identifying, 8, 178
  opening, 8
FONTALT system variable, 176
fonts, 176
freezing/thawing layers, 88, 158

G

geometric tolerances, 150–151
grid
  defined, 19
  setting, 19
  snapping cursor to, 140
  spacing, 79
  turning on/off, 53, 79
  using, 79–80
'GRID command, 79–80
grips
  color of, 50
  defined, 21
  displaying, 21, 49–50
  hot, 22
  size of, 50
  using, 22
GROUP command, 54, 80
groups, 80, 172

H

HATCHEDIT command, 81
hatches
  associative, 53
  editing, 81
  fill mode for, 77
  patterns, 34
  previewing, 35
  properties, copying, 35
  selection methods, 172
  storage of, 23
help, 11, 22
HIDE command, 81
HIDEPRECISION system variable, 170

I

'ID command, 81
IMAGE command, 82
IMAGEADJUST command, 82
IMAGEATTACH command, 82
IMAGECLIP command, 82–83

IMAGEFRAME command, 83
IMAGEQUALITY command, 83
images
  brightness, contrast, fade of, 82
  clipping, 82–83
  frames, turning on/off, 83
  mirror, 99–100, 173
  quality display, 83
  raster, 82, 172
IMPORT command, 83–84
importing
  DXF files, 71–72
  material libraries, 98
  other file formats, 83–84
insertion points, 16, 32, 33–34
INSNAME system variable, 175
INTERFERE command, 84–85
Internet browsers, opening, 38–39
INTERNET UTILITIES commands, 85–86
INTERSECT command, 86
intersections
  editing, 101
  region creation from, 135–136
islands, 37
isolines, 170–171
ISOLINES system variable, 170, 171
isometrics
  planes, selecting, 87
  turning on/off, 53
'ISOPLANE command, 87

L

LASTANGLE system variable, 174
LASTPOINT system variable, 174
LASTPROMPT system variable, 174
'LAYER command, 11, 87–88
layers
  attaching materials by, 130
  changing, 13, 48
  color and, 49
  creating, 11
  current, making, 88
  defining, 13
  deleting, 88
  freezing/thawing, 88, 158
  importance of, 13
  locking/unlocking, 88
  renaming, 53
  selecting, 88
  turning on/off, 88
  unused, removing, 120
LEADER command, 88–89
LENGTHEN command, 89–90
LIGHT command, 90–93, 126
lights
  ambient, 90, 171

Index

attenuation, 91
  color of, 92
  creating, 90–93
  distant, 92
  intensity of, 91
  modifying, 90
  position of, 91
  rendering and, 126
  spotlight, 93
'LIMITS command, 11, 93
LIMMAX system variable, 174
LIMMIN system variable, 174
LINE command, 18, 94
linear dimensions, 60, 61, 62–63
lines
  through arcs, 60
  through circles, 60
  dimension, suppressing, 172
  drawing, 94, 153
  extending, 75–76, 89–90
  freehand, 139
  infinite, 164
  parallel, 101–102
  revolving, 128
  tessellation, 201
'LINETYPE command, 94–95, 103
linetypes
  changing, 95
  continuous, through vertices of
    polyline, 113
  loading, 94–95
  plotter, 115
  scales, 94–95, 96–97
  setting, 94–95
  unused, removing, 120
LIST command, 95
LOCALE system variable, 174
LOGFILEOFF command, 96
LOGFILEON command, 96
LOGINNAME system variable, 174
'LTSCALE command, 96–97

M

MASSPROP command, 97
'MATCHPROP command, 97–98
materials, 98, 126, 129–131
MATLIB command, 98
MAXACTVP system variable, 172
MEASURE command, 98–99
MEASUREINIT system variable, 172
measurement
  distance between two points, 64–67
  object, 98–99
  units of, 55–56, 116, 172, 201
MENUECHO system variable, 174
MENUNAME system variable, 174

menus, 10
meshes
  3D, drawing, 26, 73
  3D, editing, 111–113
  exploding, 75
  ruled surface, drawing, 132–133
MINSERT command, 99
MIRROR3D command, 100
MIRROR command, 99–100
mirror images, 99–100, 173
MIRRTEXT system variable, 100, 173
MLEDIT command, 101
MLINE command, 101–102
MLSTYLE command, 102–104
model space
  switching from, 119–120
  switching to, 105
  tiled, 201
mouse, 9, 119
MOVE command, 104
moving
  base point method, 42
  dimension text, 64
  displacement method, 42, 104
  drawing display, 111
  objects, 104
MSPACE command, 105, 108
MTEXT command, 13, 68, 105–106
Multiline Text Editor, 49, 59, 61, 105–106
multilines
  defining, 101–102
  drawing, 101–102
  editing, 101
  exploding, 75
  fill mode for, 77, 103
  styles, 102–104, 120
MVIEW command, 106–107
MVSETUP command, 107–108

N

NEW command, 108
nodes, 16
Noun/Verb Selection, 21

O

object snaps
  choosing, 16
  label, 17
  location of, 17
  types of, 16
objects
  aligning, 29
  area of, calculating, 30
  breaking, 38, 65

(continued)

objects *(continued)*
  color settings for, 48–49
  copying, 42–43
  database information, listing, 95
  display order of, 66–67
  dragged, display of, 66
  erasing, 74
  information list of, 43
  moving, 104
  renaming, 52–53
  restoring, 109
  rotating, 131
  scaling, 29, 134
  selecting, 20–22, 52, 53–54, 136–137
  sorting, 54
  stretching, 145–146
OFFSET command, 108–109
OOPS command, 36, 109
OPEN command, 109–110
opening
  Aerial View windows, 20, 67
  AutoCAD, from desktop shortcut, 6
  flyouts, 8
  Internet browsers, 38–39
  new/existing drawings, 6–7, 109–110
  polylines, 112
  splines, 144
'ORTHO command, 110
'OSNAP command, 16, 110–111

P

'PAN command, 111
panning, 20, 111, 172
paper space
  defined, 20
  DWF drawings and, 70
  switching from, 105
  switching to, 119–120
parallel projection, 69–70
path curves, 128
PEDIT command, 29, 111–113
PELLIPSE system variable, 175
perimeter, 30, 97
PERIMETER system variable, 174
perspective views, 69–70
PFACEVMAX system variable, 174
pickboxes, 21, 54
PICKSTYLE system variable, 172
PLAN command, 113
plan view
  returning to, 171
  showing, 113
PLATFORM system variable, 174
PLINE command, 94, 114–115
PLINEGEN system variable, 175

PLINETYPE system variable, 175
PLOT command, 20, 115–117, 179
PLOTID system variable, 174
PLOTTER system variable, 174
POINT command, 117
point filters, 18
point light, 91
points
  accessing coordinates of, 81
  control, 143
  distance between, measuring, 64–67
  drawing, 117
  drawing at intervals, 98–100
  fit, 143, 144
  locating, 17–18
  rotating objects around, 131
  styles of, 52
polar arrays, 27
polar coordinates, 15, 19
POLYGON command, 117–118
polygons
  in 3D space, 73, 111–113
  center definition of, 118
  default number of sides, 175
  drawing, 117–118
  filled, drawing, 141
polylines
  2D, drawing, 114–115
  3D, drawing, 28–29
  arcs in, 114–115
  closing, 114
  editing, 111–113
  extending, 75–76, 89–90
  fill mode for, 77
  filleting, 77
  halfwidth of, 114
  joining, 112
  lightweight, 23, 175
  opening/closing, 112
  regenerating, 112
  revolving, 128
  smoothing, 113
  width, 112
POLYSIDES system variable, 175
precision, specifying, 170
preferences, 118–119, 132
PREFERENCES command, 118–119
printer, changing default, 174
printing, 115–117
profiles, 119
properties
  copying, 98
  mass, 97
  matching, 97–98
  object, 40, 48, 52
  region, 97

PSPACE command, 108, 119–120
puck, 9
PURGE command, 120
pyramids, drawing, 26–27

Q

QSAVE command, 8, 120
'QTEXT command, 121
QUIT command, 23, 121

R

radial dimensions, 63–64
radiuses
  arc, 63–64, 114
  circle, 63–64
  fillet, 77
raster images, 82, 172
RASTERPREVIEW system variable, 174
RAY command, 121–122
RECOVER command, 33, 122
RECTANG command, 26, 122–123
rectangles, 121, 122–123
REDO command, 123
REDRAW command, 20
'REDRAWALL command, 123–124
redrawing, 20
reflection, 129
refraction, 130
REGEN command, 20, 52, 124
REGENAUTO command, 124
REGION command, 124–125
regions
  combining, 157
  creating, 124–125
  creating from intersection, 135–136
  exploding, 75
  mass of, 97
  properties of, 97
  subtracting area of, 147
REINIT command, 125
RENDER command, 125–127
rendering
  information, listing, 145
  lights and, 126
  setting preferences for, 129–131
  windows, 126
  resolution
    setting for circles/arcs, 158
    TrueType 1 font, 176
REVOLVE command, 127–128
REVSURF command, 128–129, 171
right angles, 19, 20
RMAT command, 129–131
ROTATE3D command, 131–132

ROTATE command, 131
rotating
  around axis, 131–132
  around points, 131
  UCS, 155
roughness, 129
RPREF command, 132
RTDISPLAY system variable, 172
ruled surface, 132–133
RULESURF command, 132–133, 171
Running Object Snap modes, 110

S

SAVE command, 133
SAVEAS command, 133
SAVEFILE system variable, 174
SAVEIMG command, 133–134
SAVENAME system variable, 174
saving
  automatically, 8, 119
  drawings, 120, 133
  rendered images, 133–134
  UCS, 155
  under new file name, 133
  viewports, 161
SCALE command, 134
scaling objects, 29, 107, 134
SCENE command, 126, 134–135
SCREENSIZE system variable, 175
SECTION command, 135–136
segment length, 99
SELECT command, 21, 54, 136–137
selecting objects
  basic description of, 20–22
  controlling, 53–54
  Noun/Verb Selection and, 21
  options for, 21
'SETVAR command, 138
SHADE command, 138
SHADEDGE system variable, 171
SHADEDIF system variable, 170
shading, 125–127, 138, 171
shadows, 126
SHPNAME system variable, 175
SKETCH command, 139
SKPOLY system variable, 175
SLICE command, 139–140
smoothing angle, 126
snap
  defined, 19
  modes, setting, 110–111
  turning on/off, 53
'SNAP command, 140
SOLID command, 141

solids
  2D, creating, 127–128, 141
  3D, creating, 76, 142
  combining, 157
  creating from overlapping area, 84–85, 86
  exploding, 75
  fill mode for, 77
  filleting, 78
  hiding lines of, 81
  mass of, 97
  properties of, 97
  slicing, 139–140
  subtracting volume of, 147
  wedge, 163
sorting objects, 54
spatial index, 175
spell checking, 141–142
'SPELL command, 141–142
SPHERE command, 142
spherical coordinates, 16
SPLFRAME system variable, 175–176
SPLINE command, 142–143
SPLINEDIT command, 143–144
splines
  defined, 113
  drawing, 142–143
  editing, 143–144
  line segments, number of, 176
  opening/closing, 144
  types of, 176
SPLINESEGS system variable, 176
SPLINETYPE system variable, 176
spotlights, 93
Start Up dialog box, 6, 12, 118
STATS command, 145
status bar, 7, 10
'STATUS command, 145
STRETCH command, 145–146
'STYLE command, 11, 45, 68, 146–147
styles
  dimension, 13, 50–51, 120
  multiline, 102–104, 120
  point, 52
  text, 13, 120, 146–147, 176
stylus, 9
SUBTRACT command, 147
surfaces
  3D, 28, 81
  Bezier, 176
  blending colors across, 126
  creating by revolving, 128–129
  density, 171
  hiding lines of, 81
  ruled, 132–133
  tabulated, 149
SURFTAB1 system variable, 171

SURFTAB2 system variable, 171
SURFTYPE system variable, 176
SURFU system variable, 171
SURFV system variable, 171
system variables. *See also individual system variables*
  changing, 138
  setting values for, 138
  using, 170

T

TABLET command, 147–148
TABSURF command, 149, 171
tabulated surface, 149
TDCREATE system variable, 175
templates
  choosing, 6, 12
  creating, 46–47
  customizing, 11–12
  default, 11
  defined, 11
  list of, 12
temporary files, 175
TEMPPREFIX system variable, 175
text
  aligning, 68
  creating paragraph, 105–106
  dimension, 62, 64
  drawing, 68
  editing, 49
  height, 32, 68
  insertion point, 32
  line, creating, 149
  mirroring, 173
  options, specifying, 45
  rotation angle of, 32
  spell checking, 141–142
  styles, 13, 146–147, 176
  system variables, 176
  turning into rectangles, 121
  window contents, recording, 96
TEXT command, 149
Text Editor, 58
TEXTQLTY system variable, 176
TEXTSIZE system variable, 176
TEXTSTYLE system variable, 176
tiled viewports, 161–162
TILEMODE system variable, 106, 107, 119–120, 158
'TIME command, 149–150
TOLERANCE command, 150–151
TOOLBAR command, 8, 11, 25, 151–152
toolbars
  creating, 152
  displaying, 8, 151

docking/floating, 151–152
hiding, 151
managing, 151–152
naming, 152
ToolTips, 178
TORUS command, 152
TRACE command, 153
Tracking, 17–18
TRANSPARENCY command, 153
transparent commands, 9–10
TREEDEPTH system variable, 175
TREEMAX system variable, 175
triangles, 27
TRIM command, 153–154

U

U command, 109, 154
UCS command, 14, 154–155
UCS toolbar, 54–55, 187
UCSFOLLOW system variable, 171
UCSICON command, 156
UNDO command, 109, 156–157
UNION command, 157
units of measurement, 55–56, 116, 172
User Coordinate System (UCS)
  creating, 14, 155
  defining, 55
  deleting, 55, 155
  icon management, 156
  listing, 155
  managing, 154–155
  plan view, 113
  preset, changing, 55
  renaming, 55
  saving, 54–55, 155

V

VIEWCTR system variable, 175
viewpoints
  on compass, 161
  creating, 57
viewports
  active, 161, 162
  aligning, 107
  center of, 175
  creating, 107
  deleting, 107
  floating, 106–108, 158–160
  freezing/thawing layers in, 158–160
  joining, 161
  maximum number of, 172
  restoring, 107
  saving, 161
  scaling objects in, 107
  size of, 175
  specifications for, 107–108
  tiled, 161–162
  turning on/off, 106
  views, 162
VIEWRES command, 158
views
  3D angle, 57–58, 160–161
  creating, 56
  deleting, 56
  naming, 56
  parallel projection, 69–70
  perspective, 69–70
  plan, 113, 171
  saving, 70
  updating, 67
  viewport, 162
VISRETAIN system variable, 172
VPLAYER command, 158–160
VPOINT command, 55, 57, 81, 160–161
VPORTS command, 161–162
VSMAX system variable, 175
VSMIN system variable, 175

W

WBLOCK command, 162
WEDGE command, 163
WHIP! add-on, 71, 201
World Coordinate System (WCS), 55, 173, 175
WORLDUCS system variable, 175
WORLDVIEW system variable, 173

X

XATTACH command, 165–166
XCLIP command, 163–164
XLINE command, 94, 164
XPLODE command, 51, 164–165
XREF command, 165–166

Z

'ZOOM command, 20, 117, 167–168
zooming, 20, 168, 172

IDG BOOKS WORLDWIDE BOOK REGISTRATION

We want to hear from you!

Visit **http://my2cents.dummies.com** to register this book and tell us how you liked it!

- Get entered in our monthly prize giveaway.
- Give us feedback about this book — tell us what you like best, what you like least, or maybe what you'd like to ask the author and us to change!
- Let us know any other ...*For Dummies*® topics that interest you.

Your feedback helps us determine what books to publish, tells us what coverage to add as we revise our books, and lets us know whether we're meeting your needs as a ...*For Dummies* reader. You're our most valuable resource, and what you have to say is important to us!

Not on the Web yet? It's easy to get started with *Dummies 101*®: *The Internet For Windows*® *95* or *The Internet For Dummies*®, 5th Edition, at local retailers everywhere.

Or let us know what you think by sending us a letter at the following address:

...*For Dummies* Book Registration
Dummies Press
7260 Shadeland Station, Suite 100
Indianapolis, IN 46256-3945
Fax 317-596-5498